MAKING YOUR
BUSINESS COMPETITIVE

MAKING YOUR BUSINESS COMPETITIVE

**David Jacobs and
Alfred Homburger**

KOGAN
PAGE

To my great loves: Tamar and Mia

David Jacobs

First published in Great Britain in 1990 by Kogan Page Limited, 120 Pentonville Road, London N1 9JN.

British Library Cataloguing in Publication Data

A CIP record for this book is available from the British Library.

ISBN 0-7494-0099-4

Typeset by the Castlefield Press Limited, Wellingborough, Northants.
Printed and bound in Great Britain by
Richard Clay (The Chaucer Press), Bungay

Contents

Chapter 1

Introduction

There is an urgent need to improve business competitiveness in the face of ever-increasing global competition. Competitiveness includes two elements: the desire and the ability to compete. The desire to compete is an attitude of mind, which must be shared by all members of top management, and communicated to everybody in the company. If top management lacks this attitude, wallows in complacency, laziness or ignorance, very little will happen. We do not know how to galvanize inept top managers. We are therefore addressing those managers who do have the right attitude, but who may feel that their companies' ability to compete could be improved.

We believe that the ability to compete has two components:

- organisational efficiency
- organisational effectiveness.

The terms 'efficient' and 'effective' are used very loosely and often inter-changeably. Strictly speaking, 'efficient' means performing tasks with a minimum of effort and cost, whereas 'effective' means the ability to achieve results. It is possible to be efficient by carrying out certain tasks quickly and at low cost. However, if those tasks should not have been undertaken at all, because they do not contribute to the achievement of organizational objectives, or if the way in which they have been performed has not had the necessary impact ('going through the motions'), the organization or person performing those tasks cannot be defined as effective.

For brevity, we have elected to use the single term 'productivity' to describe the functioning of an organization or an individual, thus implying the achievement of both planned results and having impact, as well as efficiency, (cost-effectiveness), through obtaining those results in the shortest time and at minimum cost.

Achieving and maintaining organizational productivity depends on a number of factors:

- Top management's ability to define and communicate overall company objectives sufficiently clearly, so that managers at all levels can define their own departmental and personal job objectives in terms of their contribution to the achievement of company objectives.

  Clear long-term strategic objectives give a sense of direction to all employees, while clear quantified operational objectives, derived from the long-term objectives, ensure coordinated effort by all departments. Not only do clear objectives provide the starting point for better planning, they also provide unambiguous criteria for success, in terms of which each manager can measure his or her own performance.

- Top management's willingness to expand the jobs of all managers so as to give them the greatest sense of challenge and freedom of action.

- Top management's ability to develop a team of managers who constantly strive to improve their own productivity, by focusing on 'value-added' work; and a workforce that 'really cares': cares about 'getting it right first time' in accuracy, quality, cost, delivery and customer satisfaction.

- The development of operating systems which provide the most cost-effective means of planning and control and yet are suited to the human needs of managers and employees.

- Management awareness – really knowing what is going on both outside and inside the company. The focus of management attention should be on:

  ☐ The business environment, especially on markets, customers and competitors.
  ☐ Internal factors:
    — operating results (in both financial and non-financial terms);
    — the organization's structure, with particular reference to the clarity with which people understand their roles and their expected contribution;
    — the effectivess of all operating systems;
    — the working climate, which in our view is the determining factor in producing a productive organization.

- Management's ability to diagnose the symptoms disclosed both by the formal management information system and by informal personal impressions.

- Management's ability to communicate information to all levels in the organization, and to involve them in developing plans for immediate implementation and/or corrective action.

The concept of organizational productivity should be applied not only to work on the factory floor (which in many cases represents only a small proportion of total costs), but to all company activities, including the managerial. Frequently, there are opportunities for significant savings in insurance premiums, financial charges, stock levels, penalty clauses etc, which are not 'production' costs, but which have a major impact on overall costs.

Can any organization improve its competitiveness? We have no doubt that it can. The critical factor is the attitude of top management and its willingness to operate as suggested in this book. In offering these ideas, we are not presenting a theoretical treatise, or describing a utopian world. The ideas are based on our observations of the successful and less-than-successful practices of the companies with whom we have been privileged to work during three decades; they are therefore intended as practical, down-to-earth suggestions, which can be implemented in all organizations.

This book is not intended to be a textbook for students; it is rather a handbook for managers, presented in a concise form. The book's structure is intended to facilitate accessibility, and diagrams have been used where it was felt that they would contribute to better understanding of concepts.

Chapter 2

The Hierarchy of Linked Objectives

If the measure of effectiveness is the achievement of planned results, the starting point for effective action must be the definition of objectives on which to base appropriate action plans. There are two elements involved: the clarity of the objectives themselves, and the extent to which they are understood, accepted and followed by all members of the organization.

COMPANY OBJECTIVES

In the company as a whole objectives often suffer from the following short-comings:

- They are expressed only in financial terms, with no attempt to translate financial objectives into meaningful operational objectives for each division and department.

- They are set for the benefit of Stock Exchange analysts and the financial world, and do not relate to the realities of the market-place.
  We recall the resentment of a managing director, who had completed his company plans for the coming year, showing a profit projection which had been based on a very careful analysis of market potential, only to be faced by a demand from the plc chairman to add another million pounds to the profit figure.

- They are extremely vague: 'improve our image'; 'improve quality'; 'increase sales'; 'improve the working climate'. All of these are doubtless fine ambitions, but if not expressed in terms of specific targeted results, cannot serve as the focal point for effective action.

DEPARTMENTAL OBJECTIVES

At the level of divisions and departments, company objectives suffer from the following shortcomings:

- They have not been tested to ensure their feasibility, or to ensure the compatibility of the objectives of the operating departments.

We have an example in which a sales-volume objective translated into a production objective requiring three-shift working every day – a programme which would have prevented the maintenance department carrying out its essential work.

- They have been defined without the active and uninhibited participation of line managers and without a substantial measure of consensus between them.

A steel manufacturing company decided to double its productive capacity at a time when steel plants were being reduced or even closed. Half the managers believed it was a good idea, while the other half believed it was terrible. The consequence was irreconcilable conflict between the two groups.

- Managers, even at high level, are not aware of objectives.

Each manager in a major car manufacturer was asked at a seminar to write down what he believed to be the company's most important objective. The replies were sorted into almost equal groups. One group stated 'to manufacture cars and car spares'; the other group stated 'to provide jobs'. Moral considerations aside, these two objectives were incompatible, since at that time it was very difficult to sell cars. If the prime objective was to build cars only, then it would have been appropriate to reduce the workforce; had the prime objective been to provide jobs, then it would have been necessary to introduce other products. This fundamental disagreement on the very *raison d'être* of the company was a symptom of a very sick organization.

PERSONAL JOB OBJECTIVES

At the level of individual managers, lack of awareness of company and even divisional and departmental objectives leads to a lack of definition of personal job objectives, which in turn leads to work-orientation rather than results-orientation. In other words, instead of focusing on achieving objectives, the manager is anxious to show how hard he or she has worked and may even give attention to the wrong things, being unaware of real priorities. This lack of awareness of objectives and priorities leads to a lack of common understanding between managers at different levels in the organization. We know the owner of a company who took on a general manager and was subsequently very disappointed that the person had not fulfilled expectations, even though those expectations had never been defined!

CRITERIA FOR OBJECTIVES

As a starting point for effective action, objectives should fulfil the following criteria:

- *They should be specific, clear and unambiguous:*
  - the vague, unspecific 'improve our image' should read 'ensure delivery on promised dates in 95 per cent of cases; arrange press releases every month on new-product development', etc.
  - 'improve quality' should read 'reduce complaints by 50 per cent within three months; obtain the national standards institute approval on main products within six months', etc.
  - 'increase sales' should read 'increase cash sales by 15 per cent within two months, increase credit sales by 40 per cent within four months, increase number of new customers by 20 per cent within four months', etc.
  - 'improve working climate' should read 'reduce work stoppages by 10 per cent and reduce absenteeism by 25 per cent, both within three months; introduce weekly team briefings in the factory immediately'.

- *They should be measurable.* All objectives should be quantified in terms of targeted results (for example sales), which should be increased by a stated amount, or undesired results (for example accidents), which should be decreased by a stated amount; or in terms of cost. Certain objectives (for example, those relating to the working climate or to company image) may have to be expressed in terms of symptoms (absenteeism or labour turnover), or appropriate actions (team briefings or press releases). This is an essential requirement, since what is not measurable cannot be controlled.

- *They should be defined within a clear time-frame.* Objectives which have no target date are only statements of good intention and cannot form the basis for meaningful action plans. Thus, 'We will start exports to South America' is meaningless; 'We will export 10 000 pairs of shoes per month to Bolivia by 30 November' is meaningful, since it provides a focal point for all departments concerned.

- *They should be challenging,* representing something to strive for and so providing a sense of direction and excitement. They must, however, be established and accepted by the managers who will be responsible for achieving them.

  We conducted a strategic planning workshop with the managers of a small manufacturing company, who agreed that their main objective was to become the biggest in their industry. In order to do so they had to increase their sales by a multiple of ten. They analysed the implications of this outrageous objective, broke them down by departments and by time periods and decided that they could do it within five years. They then defined the sales volume required in the first year of the five-year programme, and the sub-objectives for each department in order to reach that first-year figure. Each manager then committed himself to achieving his objectives by actually signing the flip-chart paper on which he had written them. In a letter, the managing director later told us, 'I have had comments from every person who attended the workshop, ranging from "I see things differently now" to "This is like a new company". I believe that the motivation and drive that has come out of this workshop is a direct result of the way we sat down and formulated what we are going to do for the next five years. We have update meetings every two weeks; we review our actual position with the plan. Every person in the company now has a mutually agreed objective which is reviewed quarterly.'

We recently conducted the first annual follow-up workshop, when the managers reported that they had comfortably exceeded the first-year objective, thus proving to themselves that they were really on target, with every chance of meeting their ultimate objective.

- *All company, divisional and departmental objectives must be integrated into a mutually consistent hierarchy of objectives.*

THE HIERARCHY OF OBJECTIVES

The concept of a hierarchy of objectives is illustrated in Figure 2.1. Quite simply, it suggests that corporate objectives, expressed properly in financial terms, should be translated into operating objectives by each divisional or departmental chief and tested for feasibility and compatibility between them. Each divisional or departmental chief should then discuss the objectives of the unit with his or her subordinate managers, translating the unit objectives into sub-unit objectives and testing them in the same way for feasibility and compatibility. In turn, each of the subordinate managers repeats the exercise with his or her people. This sequence, as suggested by the downward-pointing arrows, is a 'top-down' method of planning. However, as suggested by the upward-pointing arrows, it envisages an upward flow of reaction and comment, which could even result in a modification of higher-level objectives.

This concept also clarifies the question of how different people are involved in the planning process. Lower-level managers are not involved in the process of setting corporate objectives; they are, however, actively involved in defining the objectives of their units in terms of company requirements, with the very real possibility that their input could change company objectives.

During a recent objective-setting workshop with the senior managers of a shipyard, we asked one of the managers if he could define his objectives. His reply was, 'I think my objectives are as follows . . . '. To our incredulous question, 'You think or you know?', he answered in all seriousness, 'I think.' The workshop helped the managers considerably to define their objectives very specifically and to 'know' them. In fact, after our workshop the senior

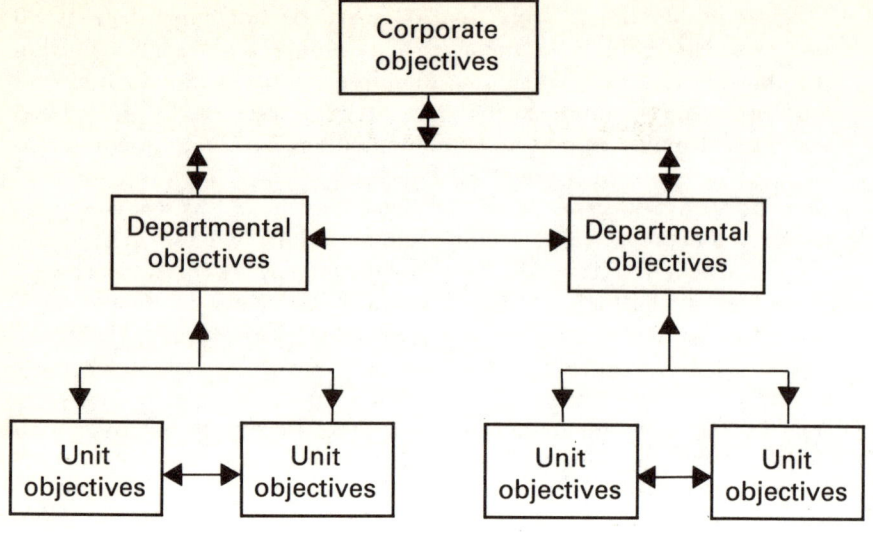

Figure 2.1   *The hierarchy of objectives*

manager repeated the exercise, involving 20 managers from different levels. They defined 132 personal job objectives (all related to the completion of a ship by a certain date), and developed a control system on a personal computer to follow up the achievement of these objectives.

Chapter 3

The Manager's Role

The object of organizational planning is to define the tasks of and relationships between divisions, departments and sections, and between the managers who are in charge of them. The document which is intended to describe these tasks and relationships is usually the organization chart (see Figure 3.1 for a typical example). This chart does show the hierarchical relationships (who reports to whom), but it gives no indication at all of the nature of each person's tasks, nor of the formal working relationships between them. Thus, while charts like this can give an overall picture of an organization's structure, they can do no more than that.

ROLE: THE IMPORTANCE OF DEFINITION

The relationship between a person and the organization in which he or she is employed is defined by that person's role. In the case of a manual worker or operator, this relationship is easily defined by the work itself: driving a truck or operating a machine. However, when the person has been promoted to a supervisory position and is responsible for the work of other people, the role is no longer so obvious. The truck driver is no longer supposed to drive a truck, but to plan and control the work of a group of drivers. This transition is very difficult. The promotion may not be to the person's liking: he may not even have been asked if he was interested in being a supervisor – many are not. He may well have been promoted because he was such a good driver and not because he showed managerial potential. The consequence is that the company has lost a good driver and failed to gain a good manager. Even if he is pleased with his new position, he has probably not been given any idea of what his new supervisory duties are, or of the distinction between managerial and operational activities. The operational area is the one he knows best and the one in which he feels most secure and self-assured, whereas the managerial area represents the unknown, calling for skills which he may not have. Operations are immediate, practical and real, while managerial activities are future-oriented and conceptual, requiring thought rather than action and often dealing with the behaviour and feelings of other people.

15

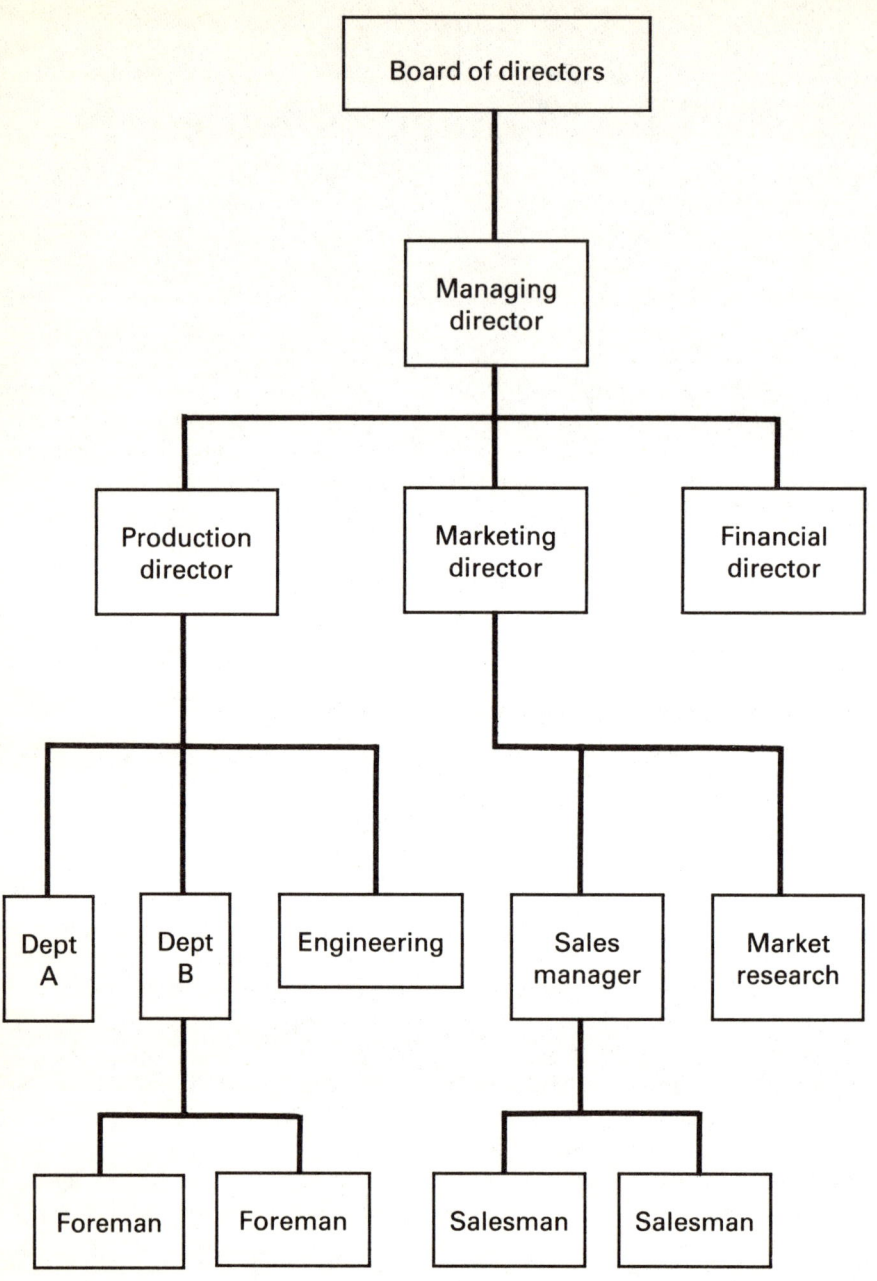

Figure 3.1 *A typical organization chart*

All of this is rather daunting, so the perfectly natural tendency of the newly appointed supervisor is to hold on to the things he knows and likes best, namely, operational details, instead of 'letting go' and concentrating on the managerial side of his job. The new manager now finds himself in a 'role set' (Figure 3.2), in which various people have expectations of his behaviour: his superior expects him to ensure that the work of the unit is done effectively and also to start taking responsibility for some of the superior's tasks; his subordinates expect him to remain their friend and to look after their interests; his peers, managers on his level in other departments, expect his collaboration in their common interest; and people in staff positions who have no formal authority over him (for example, accountants) expect him to comply with their requests. His perception of the correct priorities may well be very different from those of these other people and, in the absence of any guidelines, he will be unable to function effectively.

MANAGEMENT GUIDELINES

In many organizations no guidelines are provided at all, nor is there any management training. When a manager is promoted, he or she takes any bad working habits into the new job, and may continue to focus on the wrong things and involve himself/herself in operational details. We once carried out

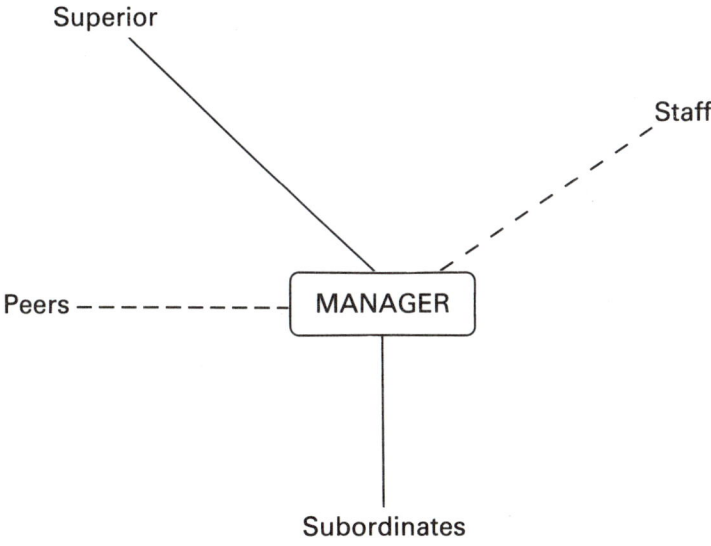

Figure 3.2   *A role set*

17

an assignment for a textile company whose president-owner had invited us to 'examine the management systems in the company'. It very quickly became apparent that the main problem was the president-owner himself, who was unable to delegate and who regarded himself as the most knowledgeable person in the company on textile machinery. (He was, in fact, because he would not teach or permit anyone else to learn.) Whenever a machine broke down, he (dressed in his president-owner suit) was always the one to get under the machine to find out what was wrong. His employees said to us, 'The boss doesn't know the value of his own time.'

The formal job description

In some organizations an attempt is made to provide guidelines through formal job descriptions. These documents tend to be long, detailed descriptions of every task the job-holder has to perform. They are time-consuming to prepare, soon out of date, emphasize work not results, are resented by the job-holders as putting them in a straitjacket and limiting their flexibility, and regarded disparagingly by senior managers who say that subordinates will not perform any activity not specifically stated in their job descriptions. A job description does not help the job-holder do his or her job better. Furthermore, since it does not represent a clear agreement between the job-holder and his or her boss as to what is acceptable performance, it cannot serve as the basis for any valid performance evaluation. At a management seminar, a manager from a bank said, 'I am embarrassed by all this talk about job descriptions. I inherited mine from my previous boss and have not looked at it for ten years.' Whereas job descriptions are inappropriate as working tools, they are useful as 'job specifications' in advertising vacant positions and in selecting candidates.

The personal annual job-plan

There is clearly a need for 'role clarification' to answer the question, 'What should I achieve?' rather than, 'What should I do?'. This process should result in a document called a 'personal annual job-plan': a personal plan, developed by the job-holder for the coming year, stating what he or she undertakes to achieve. Since the plan is personal, it is not a standard document imposed on the job-holder by the boss or the personnel department. Since it is annual, it will be prepared anew every year.

The personal annual job-plan should include the following elements.

- *Personal job objectives* which have been derived from the objectives of the job-holder's organizational unit, which in turn have been derived from the objectives of his or her department.
- *Key result areas* Those areas of activity in which results must be demon-

strated, which support the achievement of the defined objectives. These key result areas include both managerial activities (planning, organizing and controlling as well as human resource management: leading, team-building and subordinate development) and operational activities.

- *Standards of performance* A definition of the level of acceptable performance in every key result area. This level will be made mandatory by the objectives. The concepts of key result areas and of standards of performance will be discussed later in this chapter.

- *Decision-making authority* for all types of decisions, not only those relating to spending limits. This subject will be developed further in Chapter 4, *Managerial Job Design*.

- *Formal working relationships* These are very clear definitions of every key result area or every task within a key result area. They identify which person or persons (whether in the same organizational unit or another):

  — actually performs the task (acts);
  — makes the decision (decides);
  — must be consulted before the decision is made or before the task is performed;
  — must be informed of the consequences of the decision or of the performance of the task.

  This approach to defining formal working relationships recognizes that the implication of performing work or making decisions is multi-dimensional, that is, it involves other people, both within the same department and in others.

The importance of clear definition of decision-making power and formal working relationships was evident when we were invited by an American merchandising company to investigate the sources of conflict at their New York head office. Prior to our visit, we sent them a form headed, 'Who is responsible for what?' (Figure 3.3), with clear instructions: the personnel director was to prepare a master copy on which 20 typical decisions or actions were listed down the left side of the page, in the column headed 'Action or decision'; and across the top, were the initials of the various head-office people involved in making those decisions or carrying out those actions. Photocopies of the prepared form were given to 40 senior people, who were asked to complete it without consulting others. For every decision or action, they were required to indicate by a code letter the role of each person whose initials appeared at the top. These were the code letters used.

A: *Acts*
D: *Decides*
C: *Must be consulted before.*
I: *Must be informed after.*

Action or decision	Who								
	A	B	C	D	E	F	G	H	I

Figure 3.3 *Who is responsible for what?*

When we arrived in New York, we analysed the 40 completed forms and found (not to our surprise) that they were all different! When pressed for a clear definition of 'Who is responsible for what?', nobody really knew. In fact, this was the basis for the conflict: when we conducted a workshop with a group of the managers to review our findings, the typical remark was, 'That's my job, not yours', or 'I make that decision, you don't'. After much blood-letting, the group produced a new version of the form which represented a clear agreement on their individual roles.

KEY RESULT AREAS

Key result areas are a very useful concept in defining the specific tasks which have to be performed in order to achieve an agreed objective. In the previous chapter, we discussed the difficulties of defining objectives in a clear and unambiguous way. We must now look for a way to link tasks with objectives.

For certain objectives it is easy to define tasks. For example, if the defined objective of the sales manager is 'to increase sales by 15 per cent within two months', some of the relevant tasks could be defined as follows:

1. Prepare a list of potential customers in the south-east by 15 January.
2. Define new geographical areas for each salesman by 31 January.
3. Ensure availability of promotional material for distribution to potential customers by 31 January.

On the other hand, if the objective of the business development manager is 'to submit four proposals for new ventures every three months', it might be helpful first to define key results areas, such as the following:

1. Maintain regular contact with academic and research institutions.
2. Subscribe to leading international research journals.
3. Attend international research congresses.

Then, within each area, it would be possible to define the necessary tasks. Thus in relation to the first key result area (contact with research institutions), some of the tasks might be:

1. Identify institutions active in research in the following areas . . . by 31 January.
2. Obtain information on their research programmes by 28 February.
3. Establish personal contact with the director of research of each of the relevant research programmes by 15 March.

In fact, the business development manager of a Spanish chemical company followed these steps and found that defining key result areas was a very useful 'stepping stone' between defining his overall objective and defining his actual tasks.

The definition of tasks must be rigorous in clarifying and emphasizing outputs or results, and not the work itself; and the results must be expressed in measurable terms. It is measurable results which provide the basis for standards of performance, which in turn serve as criteria in evaluating managerial performance.

MANAGERIAL STANDARDS OF PERFORMANCE

In order to ensure that planned objectives are being achieved, and that managers are focusing their attention on the correct priorities, it is necessary to conduct periodic evaluations of their performance. Measuring individual performance systematically and on a regular basis (say, once every three months) has the salutory effect of:

- Reminding the manager that he will be subject to review.

- Emphasizing to the manager that he is accountable for all results of his unit (both good and bad).

- Continuously focusing on the achievement of objectives.

The basis for such performance evaluations must be measurable criteria which are directly related to the objectives of the company, and understood and accepted as valid by the manager.

The concept of performance evaluation in not a new one and is widely practised in both the private and the public sectors. However, it is usually used to assess a person, not in terms of measurable results but in terms of personal characteristics and behaviour, which are neither measurable in objective terms nor in any way related to the achievement of objectives. It is interesting and diverting to look at part of the performance evaluation forms of the army of a world power and of companies owned by the government of a certain European country (Figure 3.4).

In the case of the army, the reviewing military officer or senior manager on the administrative side was supposed to assess his subordinate, in terms of each performance quality, by selecting the verbal description which most closely matched his opinion. We found the possibility of describing a person's 'behaviour . . . off duty' as 'exceeds duty requirements' a very intriguing one. Assuming the senior was aware of the subordinate's off-duty behaviour, what were 'duty requirements' and was there a common understanding of what they should be? Furthermore, what did this evaluation have to do with the results of the subordinate's activities on the job, namely the results he should achieve? (We are pleased to report that this system had now been replaced with a system of standards of performance based on measurable results.)

In the case of the government-owned companies, the form defines the performance criteria (all irrelevant to results); and then merely describes the worst and the best cases, providing a numerical scale (8 to 16) between the two extremes. Our only comment on this form is that we find it hilarious. If 'dogmatic' means 'based on *a priori* principles, not on induction' and also 'asserting a matter of opinion as if it were fact' and if 'pragmatic' means 'practical, matter of fact' and also 'dealing with events in such a manner as to show their interconnection', then we would ask 'At what point on the scale does 'dogmatic' become 'pragmatic'? And what would your reaction as a subordinate be if your boss stated that you were 'notoriously deficient and confused'?

The use of such forms puts the superior in an invidious position, since he

Army

Performance qualities	Ranks with the very best	Superior to most	Exceeds or meets duty require-ments	Needs improve-ment
Takes pride in high standards of dress, grooming and military manner (military bearing).				
Behaviour on and off duty is in accordance with highest Army standards (personal conduct).				

Government-owned companies

Performance criteria	4	8 12 16	20
Quantity of work	Slow. Output notoriously insufficient.		Exceptionally fast. Great capacity for work.
Quality of work	Frequent errors.		Precise.
Flexibility	Dogmatic.		Pragmatic.
Verbal ability	Notoriously deficient and confused.		Exceptionally fluent and clear.
Social contact	Difficult.		Naturally simple and social.

Figure 3.4 *Extracts from two performance evaluation forms*

or she is compelled to make subjective judgements in terms of almost meaningless criteria.

For standards of performance to be meaningful and relevant to both the job-holder and his or her boss, they should satisfy the following criteria:

- They should represent an agreement, in advance, between the job-holder and the boss about what is acceptable performance in every key result area. There should be no surprises – everybody is entitled to know how he or she is going to be assessed.

- They should measure results of managerial performance in terms of:
  — quantity,
  — quality,
  — time,
  — cost.

- The acceptance levels of performance should be derived from the objectives of the company, and should be proposed by the job-holder and accepted by the boss. (They should not be imposed by the boss and reluctantly accepted by the subordinate. We do believe, however, that if there is an irreconcilable difference between boss and subordinate, the boss's judgement should prevail.) The standards of performance should be:
  — quantified,
  — fact-based,
  — challenging yet achievable,
  — fair,
  — understood,
  — acceptable.

Standards of performance which are set up in the way described will serve as the basis for:

- Self-control (that is, self-management) by the job-holder.
- Performance-evaluation by the job-holder's boss.

Conducting performance evaluations in a positive and supportive way, in order to help the job-holder improve his or her performance, will be discussed in Chapter 5.

The topics which have been described in this chapter are the component parts of a coherent concept of management (Figure 3.5). Throughout the entire organization, this concept is results-oriented rather than work-oriented and supports the achievement of planned objectives.

- Company objectives are translated into operational objectives for each department.
- Departmental objectives are in turn translated into operational objectives for each organisational unit within the department.

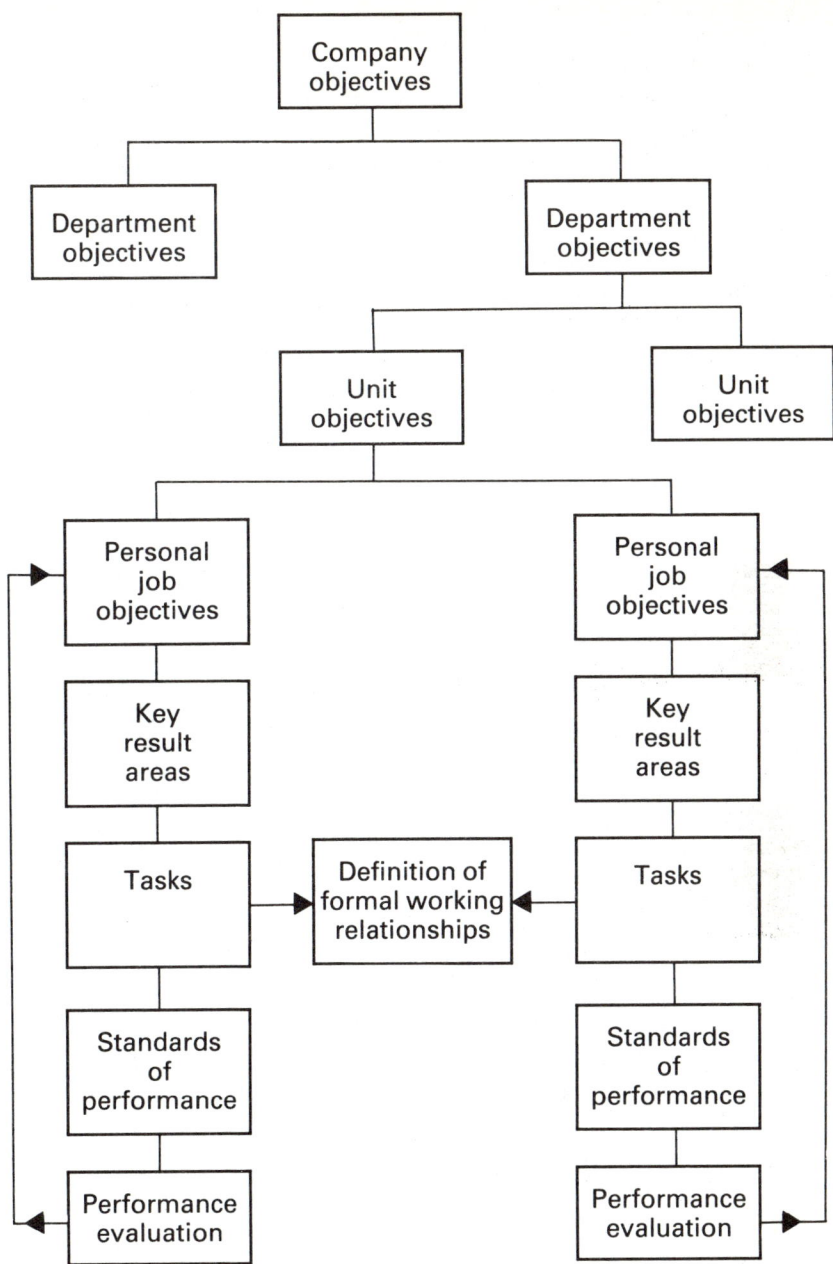

Figure 3.5 *A results-oriented concept of management*

- The manager of each unit within the department derives his or her personal job objectives from the objectives of the unit for which he or she is responsible. A rigorous check is made to ensure that the personal job objectives of all unit managers are compatible, and that the achievement of these personal objectives will ultimately result in the achievement of the objectives of the department.
- Each manager defines his or her key result areas and specific tasks in terms of his or her personal job objectives.
- Quantified standards of performance are agreed between each manager and the respective boss, defining levels of performance which are acceptable in terms of the objective requirements of the unit and the department.
- Periodical performance evaluation discloses those areas in which improvement is necessary, resulting in the definition of new or additional personal job objectives.

Chapter 4

Managerial Job Design

The source of energy for the achievement of company objectives is obviously the workforce, and in particular the managers. Yet it is a common phenomenon that, whereas so much is expected of managers, so little is done to tap into the source of energy which they represent. Essentially what each of us wants at work is:

- *Opportunity* to deal with challenging assignments and interesting material, and to perform to the best of our ability.

- *Autonomy* in the way we work; a sense of control over what we do and how we do it.

In many cases poor job structure and a lack of understanding of people's basic needs leave managers frustrated and even bored.

These two elements must be dealt with separately even though both derive from the process of delegation. Opportunity relates to job-content, whereas autonomy relates to the way in which decision-making power is defined. When a senior manager designs the job of a subordinate manager, he or she is in fact delegating work and a measure of decision-making power relating to that work.

DELEGATING WORK (OPPORTUNITY)

Unfortunately, the process of delegation is often done badly. The delegated work is usually relatively uninteresting – part of the senior's job which he or she would like to get rid of, or a series of specific tasks which the senior feels are 'simple enough' for the subordinate to deal with. In the latter case the instruction is usually, 'When you have finished the task, come back to me and, if you've done it right, I'll give you another.' The message is obvious: 'I do not trust you sufficiently to do a larger piece of work, so will keep control of you by giving you these small pieces to do, one at a time.'

We have seen how giving a subordinate a 'real' job to do produced the most dramatic results. Some years ago we were involved in an extensive programme of management development with administrative, service and support units of the United States Army in West Germany. A workshop on 'improving performance' included practical projects which were selected by the participants. One participant, who had undertaken a project on 'improving job-satisfaction in my unit', described himself as a senior construction engineer, responsible for the design of housing for military personnel and their families. His direct subordinates were two much older German engineers, employed by the US Army. Prior to starting the job-satisfaction project he had delegated work as described earlier, giving his subordinates very small design assignments which he would check very carefully before giving the next assignment. Needless to say, the productivity of his unit was very low. After the project he took the daring step of calling in his two subordinates and, to their amazement, suggested that they undertake the design of a complete housing estate and bring the design to him for review when it was completed. By his description, the results were extraordinary, not only in the obvious pleasure the subordinates got from their assignment, but also in the quality of the design and the speed with which it was completed.

We believe that this example of delegating a 'whole' task rather than a series of fragmented tasks is significant. In too many organizations employees are 'work-oriented' rather than 'results-oriented'. In other words, people believe that the important thing is to prove how hard they have worked, rather than showing the results they have achieved. A process of delegation which assigns only specific tasks will serve to reinforce work-orientation. What is required is a process of delegation which reinforces a results-orientation, hence the slogan 'Delegate objectives, not work', which is exactly what the young American engineer did.

Of course, there is a whole range of possibilities in delegating and supervising work. One extreme is minimal delegation and 'breathing down the necks' of subordinates. This kind of close supervision might possibly be appropriate for new employees, but will certainly generate resentment in them. The superior can step back from the detail of the work and only ask to see completed sections, at predetermined due-dates (milestones). He or she can step back even further and review completed projects only. There is a further possibility, which is tantamount to abdication, whereby the superior will indicate no standards of performance, no deadlines, and will not make it clear to the subordinates that they will be subject to review. (This last case is described somewhat tongue-in-cheek, though we can certainly remember similar situations in real life.) The position of a superior on this continuum will depend on the capabilities of his or her subordinates. We suggest that most subordinates are capable of much more than we give them credit for, and that the position of the superior should be to step back as far as possible (but without abdicating!).

DELEGATING DECISION-MAKING POWER (AUTONOMY)

The other aspect of delegation relates to decision-making power. We can distinguish the following possibilities.

1. *There is no delegation of decision-making authority.*

This applies particularly to middle management, which is also denied information about the direction and objectives of the company. The consequences of this kind of management can be total alienation.

We had an object lesson in the case of a very large steel manufacturer, by whom we were asked to conduct a management audit to identify problem areas. This was a company with a history of bad labour relations, managed by 'remote control' by a president and a board of directors who conducted strategic planning sessions in a neighbouring country so that their decisions would be kept secret, and who issued directives to the company in the name of communication. We never understood why they invited us at all, and warned the board that in starting such a project they would have a 'tiger by the tail' in the participating managers' expectations for change. They assured us that they were aware of this and were prepared to make the necessary changes. One thousand managers were asked to complete our questionnaire and, in a gesture of absolute alienation, 650 refused to do so. We analysed the 350 replies received by using a computer program which printed out 'profiles' of the perceptions of the respondents, once 'vertically' for each of five factories and eight staff departments, and once 'horizontally' for each of three levels of management, irrespective of the organization unit. The findings were consistent: 12 of the 13 units defined the major problem as 'lack of motivation'. The horizontal profiles showed clearly that the perceptions of middle management were significantly more negative than those of the other two groups. The sequel to this story proves its point: despite the overwhelming evidence of our report and our detailed recommendations, nothing at all was done. If anything, the consequences created even more hostility.

We have also a ludicrous example of the extremes to which a combination of lack of delegation and bureaucratic procedures can lead. While working in a large government-owned company we were told by a third-level manager that he had the authority to sign certain outgoing letters. In his department he had a bright subordinate to whom he delegated the right to sign these letters. Unfortunately, the first time the subordinate did sign, the letters were returned by the mail department, who stated that since he had no authority, the letters could not be mailed. In order to delegate this task, the manager had to submit a written request to the board of directors; not to his boss on the second level in the hierarchy, but to the board! Astounded, we tackled the relevant board member with the question, and were told blithely, 'Why not, it only takes a second to sign my approval.' We returned to the manager, to be told that he had submitted his request three months previously and, since he had received no reply, had given up hope of ever being able to make a change.

2. *There is no clear definition of decision-making authority.*

Where a clear definition of decision-making authority is lacking there are serious problems for the job-holder and for his or her subordinates and peers. In the absence of a clear definition of authority, the non-assertive manager will do anything to avoid making a decision, whereas the assertive manager will make decisions which perhaps he or she should not. Subordinates are not sure to whom to turn for a decision or, alternatively, they turn to the person who will give the decision they want. With peers, there are constant conflicts over the right to make decisions. This point was referred to in Chapter 3, in connection with the American merchandising company's problems over formal working relationships (Figure 3.3).

3. *Authority is defined only for spending limits.*

The obvious drawback to this method is that many non-financial decisions are ignored.

4. *Authority is defined in a series of steps.*

- A: Things you can do and not tell your superior.
- B: Things you can do, provided you tell your superior afterwards.
- C: Things for which you must get your superior's permission first.

This sounds logical, but it is extraordinaily difficult to write down. What is perhaps more important, it is a very constricting way of defining a person's authority.

Linear responsibility charts

Even in cases where detailed job descriptions are prepared, including a comprehensive definition of the decision-making powers of the job-holders, the documents do not recognise that a manager does not operate in a vacuum, that his or her decisions and actions must be taken in conjunction with other managers, and that he or she is involved in other managers' decisions and actions. The involvement of at least four people must be defined in relation to every decision and action. These definitions are known as 'formal working relationships', referred to in Chapter 3. In the discussion on role clarification:

- Who makes the decision
- Who acts (this may be the same person who makes the decision)
- Who must be consulted before the decision is made or the action is taken.

More than one person may have to be consulted. ('Consultation' does not mean asking for permission, merely obtaining information and perhaps guidance; for example, asking the chief accountant about the income tax implications of a proposed action.)

- Who must be informed that a decision has been made, or an action taken. Again, more than one person may have to be informed. This is not a matter of getting approval, but of ensuring that essential information is passed on.

A linear responsibility chart is a convenient means of showing on a single page:

- The most important decisions and actions which are taken in an organizational unit
- The people who are involved
- The type of involvement of each person with specific decisions and actions.

Figure 4.1 (overleaf) shows a completed linear responsibility chart which defines formal working relationships. It identifies the most important decisions that have to be taken in a given organization unit and defines exactly the involvement of the various managers in each decision. On the top line are the initials of each person in the organization unit and of those outside the unit who are involved in its decision-making process. Under 'Description' is a list of the unit's most important activities. By completing the chart as a team exercise, common understanding is achieved as to the nature of the activities, and the people who must be involved are identified. In the process of completing the chart, there is often a great deal of negotiation between the team members regarding the roles they should play. If, over a period, one person displays competence in a particular area, the 'D' which was recorded in his boss's column, can be reassigned to his, indicating increased responsibility.

We have found that the use of this chart persuades authoritarian top managers that the 'Ds' should not *all* appear under their name, but should gradually shift to the columns of their subordinates.

The unit-president concept

This concept has been promoted by the American Management Association for many years. The idea is that top management should try to evoke 'presidential-type behaviour' in their subordinate managers (independent, entrepreneurial, risk-taking, with very strong self-control); that is, to be the 'President' of their organizational units. Individual managers are not told what they may or may not do, but rather that they can do anything to achieve

Responsible person (initials)		M D	F S	M P	L C	V F	D B		P C	N T	C D	J P
Task	Description											
1	Strategic Planning	D	I	A	A	A			C	C	C	C
2	Operational Planning		A D	I	I	I	I					
3.1	Organization Clarification	D	A	C	C	C	C					
3.2	Up-date Job Descriptions	D	D	A	A	A	A					
3.3	Standards of Performance	D	D	A	A	A	A					
4.1	Control: System Development	D	A									
4.2	Performance Appraisals	D	A	C	C	C	C					
5.1	Climate-Setting		A D	C	C	C	C					
5.2	Reduce Absenteeism		D	A	A	A	A					
6	Training		D	A	A	A	A					
7.11	Define Data Needs		D	I	A	I	I		C	C	C	C
7.12	Design System		D	C	C	C	A		C	C	C	C
7.13	Programming		D				A					
7.14	Implementation		D	C	C	C	A		C	C	C	C
7.21	Define Inventory Levels		D			A			C	C	C	C
7.22	Improve Data Collection		D		A				C			C
7.23	Design System		D		A				C			C
7.24	Implementation		D		A				C			C
7.31	Improve Recordings Accuracy		D	A								
7.32	Reduce Reporting Delays	D		A								
7.41	Cash-flow Projections	D	D	C		A			C	C	C	C
7.42	Analysis of Financial Report	D	D	A			A					
7.43	Analysis of Costing Report	D	D		A		A		C			
7.44	Analysis of Budgetary Control	D	D			A	A		C	C	C	C

Code   A: Acts   C: Must be consulted
       D: Decides   I: Must be informed

Confirmation on: ___/___/___
   By job holder: _____
       Superior: _____

Source: DJ Jacobs & Associates

Figure 4.1 *Linear responsibility chart*

their objectives, provided it is not on the 'No-No List'. This list includes activities forbidden by law, public interest and morality, as well as specific constraints in terms of company policy, plans, budgets and procedures. Within these boundaries, the manager can function independently in his or her 'area of decision-making freedom'. Figure 4.2 illustrates this concept: the small square in the traditional organization chart is enlarged into an 'Area of freedom', bounded by the constraints of the 'No-No List'. This is a very attractive concept for managers. To make it successful, each manager must clearly understand:

- The objectives of his or her unit
- His or her area of decision-making freedom
- That he or she will be subject to periodic review, in order to compare actual achievements with planned objectives, to determine the reasons for variances and to examine his or her plans for the future.

The linear responsibility chart (Figure 4.1) highlights the difference between traditional organization charts – which merely show a series of boxes, without any indication of the contents of the boxes or the relationship between them – and the chart that provides real information in a meaningful and challenging way. Even if the 'Unit President Concept' is adopted and areas of decision-making freedom are defined, it is still possible to use the linear responsibility chart to define decisions on the 'No-No List' which must be taken by higher-level managers and those decisions which must involve people from other departments.

ASPECTS OF JOB DESIGN

A very useful exercise in job design is to invite a group of managers to define the three things they most want from their jobs, and then to assess the extent to which they actually achieve those desires. The most common responses to the former are:

- achievement/success
- personal development
- enjoyment/fun
- recognition
- status
- power
- self-'esteem
- security
- belonging
- freedom
- making a valuable contribution

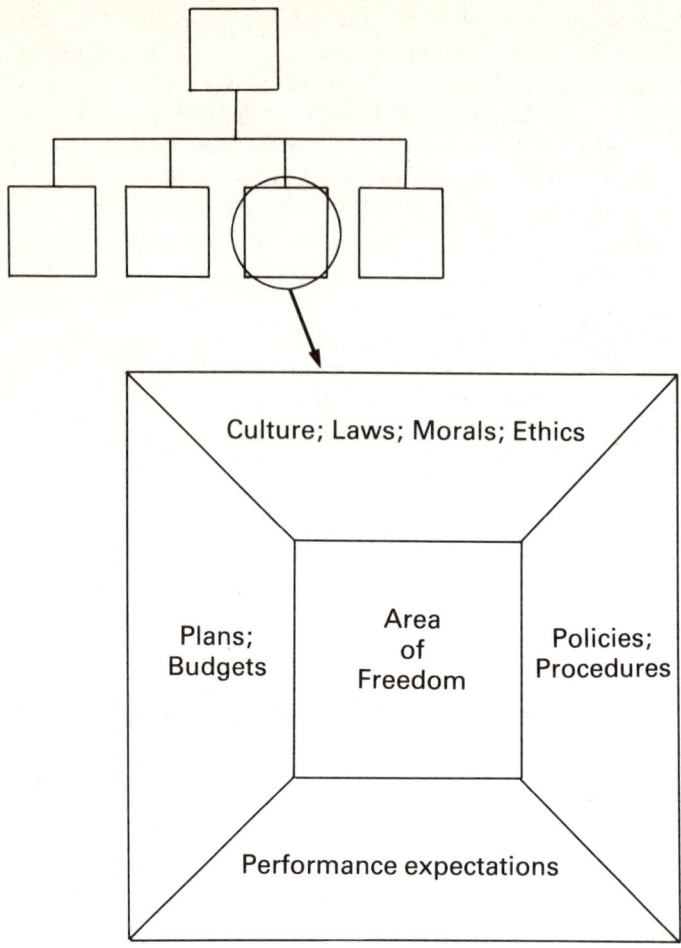

Figure 4.2 *The unit-president concept*

When asked to complete the assessment form (Figure 4.3), most people state that what they lack is 'power' (meaning autonomy) and 'recognition'. This exercise can be continued in two directions:

- Initiate an open discussion with the managers' bosses to examine ways of enabling the managers to obtain what they want.

- Ask the same group of managers what they think their subordinates want from their jobs. This question often produces an embarrassed silence, eventually broken when when somebody says, 'They want the same things that we do.' The embarrassment is the tacit admission that they have never asked the question. The next practical step is to suggest to the group that they conduct the same exercise with their subordinates:

Assess your job satisfaction Name _____			
	Degree of satisfaction		
I want my job to give me:	High	Medium	Low
Achievement/Success			
Personal development			
Enjoyment/Fun			
Recognition			
Status			
Power			
Self-esteem			
Security			
A sense of belonging			
Freedom			
A chance to make a valuable contribution			

Figure 4.3   *Assessment form*

— definition of personal desires;
— assessment of degree of satisfaction of those desires;
— discussion on how to enable them to achieve a greater degree of job satisfaction.

We worked in America with a chemical company that has developed this approach even further. They have instituted what they call 'Job-Satisfaction Circles', which meet regularly to find ways of improving job satisfaction.

What happened at a training seminar which we conducted with a group of senior managers illustrates that the perceptions that one group has of another are often totally inaccurate. When asked what they wanted from their jobs, almost unanimously the managers said, 'achievement and satisfaction'. When asked what they though junior secretaries wanted, they answered unanimously, 'money'. Later, during the same seminar, we had the

35

opportunity of asking two junior secretaries what they wanted from their jobs. As expected, both answered, 'achievement and satisfaction'. When we asked what they thought their high-powered bosses wanted, they chorused, 'Money'.

Chapter 5

Management Systems

In the beginning of this book we pointed out that an efficient organization is one which is effective, in that it achieves planned results. Despite the obvious validity of this statement, in practice, planning is not taken as seriously as might be expected.

PLANNING PROBLEMS

1. *There is no systematic business planning at all.*

Managers often claim to be 'too busy to plan', particularly in smaller companies. In fact, they are too busy, dealing with an endless series of 'life-or-death' situations; or trying to cope with the results of early success – the production department desperately trying to keep up with what the sales department has undertaken to supply. In these situations, any planning period beyond next week is simply out of sight.

Another common situation is that of the company which continues doing routinely what it has always done, and sees no reason to change (the nose to the grindstone phenomenon).

A third situation which undermines planning is when the future of a company is uncertain. The possibility of producing reliable forecasts is extremely unlikely and the prevailing attitude is usually, 'Why bother to plan? Whatever we plan to do will have to be changed anyway.'

The consequences of a lack of systematic business planning are usually:

*   Crisis-oriented responses; a 'fire-fighting' mode of operation to deal with unanticipated events.

*   Failure to take advantage of opportunities which might have been identified during the planning process.

*   Failure to anticipate threats. This point is particularly significant in relation to technological change. A successful American manufacturer of hairpins was ruined by hair spray, which is a product based on an entirely different technology (aerosols) that provides a more effective answer to

the market need. The need is for 'something' which will keep hair in place, not for hairpins. If we were to ask whether the top management of the hairpin company could be accused of failure to anticipate threats of technological change, we would probably have to admit that it was highly unlikely that they could have foreseen such an eventuality. More recently, the pressure of environmentalists has led to the need to develop an ozone-friendly hair spray. Whereas this is not a case of an entirely different technology, it is an example of the need to be responsive to external factors.

A rather different case is that of the American glass-bottle manufacturers who believed that beer would always be drunk out of glass bottles (after all, it always had been), and were caught completely by surprise when the brewers started to package beer in disposable aluminium cans. This time, if we ask whether the top management could be accused of negligence by failure to anticipate this kind of change, we believe that the answer is a resounding 'Yes'. As the Americans would say, the 'name of the game' for top management is 'anticipate and plan'. The sequel to this story is that, having blissfully ignored the aluminium-can threat, the same top managers were apparently hit again by the unanticipated appearance of plastic containers which became substitutes for some of their products.

- The misuse of resources, resulting from 'management by impulse': rushing into projects without a serious attempt to assess benefits, costs and risks, and without judgement in terms of clear criteria. We were present at a board meeting of a mining company, where a major investment (millions of dollars) in equipment was approved after super-ficial discussion. The explanation, given airily by one of the managers, was that 'at our level of turnover, these amounts are not significant'. However, the next topic on the agenda was the purchase of office equip-ment for some thousands of dollars – the discussion went on for an hour!

- Emphasis on short-term objectives at the expense of long-term benefits. In the 'trade-off' between short- and long-term objectives, the lack of a planning process which obliges managers to face these alternatives usually results in the choice of short-term benefits. Whenever there is a cash-flow or profit problem, the temptation is to postpone discretionary expenses: preventive maintenance, advertising, research and development, training.

The following quote is from an article entitled 'Companies that rob the future', which appeared in *Fortune* magazine. 'Many chief executives are jacking up profits by pouring money into quick-payoff projects and starving investments that would yield income years from now . . . they may abandon textbook analysis and follow a different rule: any project that pays off after I retire is not worthwhile.'

2. *When planning is done, it is perceived negatively by managers.*

In companies where a planning process has been imposed by a remote corporate headquarters there is resentment of the need to prepare and present a plan, which is perceived as a meaningless formality. The typical remark at planning time is, 'Let's get the plan done and delivered so that we can get back to work.' It is a curious fact that in companies like this the planned rate of growth is always 15 per cent. Somehow, 15 per cent seems to be an acceptable rate: less than 15 per cent might appear to be unambitious; more than 15 per cent would seem too rash.

Companies with remote corporate headquarters often feel that the guide-lines they are given, particularly with regard to required return on investment, are completely out of touch with reality. Plans are made by 'professional planners' (corporate planning departments or even outside consultants), who have no responsibility for achieving the planned results. The inevitable consequence is a chasm between the 'planners' and the 'doers'. We remember a shipyard where the operating managers said openly about the plans they were given, 'We tear them up and start again.'

3. *Strategic plans are not implemented.*

When the action plans for implementing the strategic plan are inadequate in each operating period, the expected results of the strategic plan will not materialize. Weak implementation plans suffer from the following shortcomings.

- They do not provide specific definitions:
    — what is to be achieved;
    — how well it must be done;
    — by when;
    — by whom;
    — at what cost.

    These definitions are of particular importance when the operation must be spread over an extended period. Not only are final objectives important, but the achievement of intermediate objectives is essential if the overall programme is to be fulfilled.

- They do not define exactly the resources that will be required:
    — man-hours (by skill group);
    — machine-hours;
    — materials;
    — funds;
    — computer time, etc.

- They do not define:
  — constraints within which the implementation will be carried out;
  — possible bottlenecks;
  — obstacles to implementation;
  — problems which might be created by the implementation of the plans.

- They do not provide for a monitoring process which will ensure that each 'milestone' is reached as planned, or that alternative action is taken if targets are not achieved. In most companies the only management information system is the financial one, reporting financial data at monthly intervals. The information required for proper follow-up of implementation plans is not in financial terms, nor is it required at monthly intervals (for example, 'Develop five new styles by 16 July' or 'Train seven salesmen to be fluent in Spanish by end October').

IMPROVING PLANNING

What is called for is a process which provides clear answers to two questions:

- Where do we want to be?
- How are we going to get there?

At this point, we cannot resist the temptation to comment on an expression which has become very popular in Britain: 'forward planning' – a useful concept, in that it makes a clear distinction between 'forward planning', 'backward planning' and 'sideways planning'!

We believe very strongly that there are two dimensions to the process of business planning:

1. *It should give a clear sense of direction, producing plans that:*

- Are based on as long-range a view as is possible.
- Are based on clearly stated assumptions about the future.
- Include projections which are not merely an extrapolation of past performance, but represent managers' best judgement of anticipated future competitive conditions.
- Provide the basis for effective action by defining quantified objectives and a time-frame.
- Describe the action plans required for implementation, including all the elements described above.
- demonstrate a clear understanding of financial criteria, including:
  — profit and return on investment;
  — cash flow;
  — balance-sheet strength.

- Provide a system of control and evaluation of group and individual performance.

2. *It should gain agreement and enthusiasm from the managers who are required to implement the plans, ie:*

- Understanding of the issues involved, the assumptions made and the implications of the plans.
- Consensus about the objectives and the means of achieving them.
- 'Ownership' of the plans – 'our' plans, not 'somebody else's' plans.
- Commitment to the achievement of the plans.

We believe that this second aspect of planning is the critical one. (Someone once said, 'It is better to have a less-than-perfect plan which everybody believes in, than a theoretically perfect plan which nobody believes in.') It can only be achieved through a process of 'team planning', in which operating managers participate in an uninhibited way, contributing both ideas and criticism.

We wish to clarify and emphasize a point made earlier: plans must be made by operating managers, not by consultants and not by professional planners from a corporate planning department. The involvement and contribution of outsiders should be as facilitators of the planning process (particularly when the operating managers have no previous experience in planning), and in the collection and analysis of data which operating managers cannot do themselves. The operating managers will use these data and analyses in drawing their own conclusions, and making their own decisions.

Because of time constraints in completing the plan, it may be that all managers (particularly supervisors) cannot be involved. It is then of the utmost importance to communicate the contents of the plan to those managers, as well as to the workforce. The disclosure of plans exposes the company to the risk of leakage to competitors. We believe that this risk can be minimized by keeping secret any parts of the plan that really do have great potential value to competitors, and presenting the rest in an appropriate degree of detail and in terms which will be understood by the employees. The very fact of disclosure is an important signal by top management of their trust in their people, and their desire to reinforce a feeling of belonging to a company which has a clear direction.

The question is often asked: 'How do we know if we have made a good plan?' This book is not a textbook on planning; there are certainly enough of those. We would suggest, however, that the following checklist could serve as the basis for a rigorous review of plans. The questions should be asked by people who were not directly involved in the planning process (perhaps non-executive directors or consultants), and the answers given by those who made the plans ('defending their thesis').

Planning checklist

1. *Environment:* Have we adequately considered all aspects of our business environment; have we identified all trends which may have an impact on us?

2. *Assumptions:* Are our assumptions reasonable or are we being unduly optimistic/pessimistic?

3. *Objectives:* Are our objectives clear and quantified?

4. *Alternatives:* Have we identified and examined sufficient alternatives?

5. *Criteria:* Have we used clear and objective criteria in selecting the best alternatives?

6. *Legality:* Are our planned activities legal?

7. *Consistency:* Are our objectives and plans consistent with our company values and policies?

8. *Realism:* Are our projected benefits and costs realistic?

9. *Implementation:* Have we given sufficient thought to the details of implementation?

10. *Time:* Have we allowed sufficient time for successful implementation?

11. *Capability:* Have we the necessary financial, physical and human resources – can we do it?

12. *Risks:* Have we considered all possible risks?

13. *Problems:* Have we identified all existing or potential problems, and do we know how we will deal with them?

To summarize, we suggest that, to be effective, a planning process must:

- be objective-oriented;
- be fact-based;
- involve all management levels;
- assign tasks and times;
- provide for controls;
- motivate – make things happen.

IMPROVING CONTROL

In considering the effectiveness of the control system in any organization, we ask three questions:

- *Does the system work?*
- *How is the control system perceived?*
- *What effect does the control system have?*

42

Let us examine each of these questions in detail.

Does the system work?

1. *Has the system been designed so that it is appropriate to the organizational structure of the company?*

In other words, does it collect data about the inputs and outputs of each department and each departmental unit so as to provide for the information needs of each operational manager? This is an appropriate question to begin our enquiry, because the organization's structure and managerial responsibilities often outgrow the original definitions on which the control system was designed. The following example of an inadequate system is from a company with which we have worked.

A steel-manufacturing company has two plants. They are geographically distant from each other, produce completely different products, supply completely different sectors of the market, and keep their own separate customer-accounts records. However, the company's general financial records, which are kept at head office, make no distinction between the two plants and produce monthly figures including all income and expenses of the two plants together. The plant managers requested that the plants be recognized as separate profit centres, that separate records be kept, and separate monthly reports prepared, to enable them to measure their performance. The chief accountant, when approached within this request, flatly refused, saying, 'Let them work it out for themselves.'

2. *Does the system provide information that is perceived as accurate by its employees,* or does it suffer from the 'garbage-in-garbage-out' syndrome?

We recall the storeman who, when asked how many units of a certain item there were in stock, calculated the balance on the back of a cigarette packet, ignoring the computer printout, which he described as 'junk'.

3. *Is relevant information made available on a regular basis to all levels of management, for purposes of planning and control, as well as for problem solving and decision making?*

From the steel manufacturer mentioned earlier, we can quote the following two examples.

The managers of the two plants were supplied with bulky monthly production reports; they used the blank reverse sides as scrap paper. Their comment was, 'It is too much, in too much detail, in a form which we cannot use.'

In this company production is continuous. The 24-hour day is divided into three shifts, each with a different shift boss. When we asked to see the report that each shift boss is given to show the results of his eight-hour period of duty we were astounded to be told that only a daily report is prepared, showing the overall results of the last 24 hours. How is it possible to make a supervisor interested in improving results, or to feel that he is at all responsible for results, when the very information he needs is withheld from him?

We suggest that the following points should be considered in designing reports for operating managers:

- Ask each manager what information he wants and in what form. We must admit, however, that there are occasional cases of managers who are unable to define their requirements. Some years ago we were working on the design of a management information system for a textile plant in northern Greece, which was about to expand its operations quite considerably. When we asked the plant manager what additional information he would require in the enlarged plant, his reply was that he did not need any – he would just walk around more often!

- Define which information should be presented in numerical and which in non-numerical form. For many people, non-numerical presentation of data is more meaningful than columns of figures.

- Consider the degree of detail which is appropriate to each level of management. The rule should be that more detail is required by lower-level managers, who are responsible for very specific activities, whereas less detail is required by higher-level managers, who are more interested in the overall picture.

- Since a very important aspect of reporting is speed of response, it is often worth forgoing a degree of accuracy in order to be able to provide information more quickly.

- To make reports meaningful to operating managers it is important to distinguish between factors which are controlled by them, and those which are not.

- The timing of reports must be defined in terms of operating needs.

4. *Does the system provide control over activities so as to prevent errors of commission or omission?*

Two quotations from the *New York Herald Tribune* are relevant here:

'The Pentagon's Inspector-General has explained how it is possible to lose $1.6 billion through waste and inefficiency:

— The Pentagon failed to charge foreign governments for the cost of improving United States fighter aircraft sold to them. Cost: $278 million.

— The Army spent $252 000 to instal new boiler systems and improve car parks in serveral buildings that were due to be demolished.

— The Naval Air Systems Command paid $27 million to repair defective weapons; repairs which the manufacturers should have carried out free of charge.
— The Navy bought $8.8 million worth of uniforms it did not need.'

'Because of chronic flaws in military bookkeeping and management, the US armed services have no idea how much military equipment is stolen or lost, the General Accounting Office has reported.'

5. *To what extent does the control system provide protection against the danger of legal action in those areas where the organization may be vulnerable?*

Legally speaking, companies most need protection against:

● product liability;
● criminal actions (committed either knowingly or unknowingly).

Here is a dramatic example to illustrate the second point. In Italy the act of employing a person directly, not through the local Labour Exchange, is defined as criminal. At the time of this story, Alfa Romeo was a government-owned car manufacturer employing some 35 000 people in two plants, one in the north and one in the south of the country. In the Alfa Sud plant, a clerk in the personnel office employed a worker illegally by bypassing the Labour Exchange. The fact became known and the president of the company, in his representative capacity, was brought to court, found guilty and resigned as a consequence. Perhaps other presidents would not have resigned, but the point is well made. The president should have instructed the legal department to identify all situations in which the company could be vulnerable; to develop appropriate control mechanisms; and, in the event of such a situation occurring anyway, to disclose and report on it as soon as possible.

How is the control system perceived?

1. *Is the system used to control people, or to measure results?*

In organizations where the system is used to control people the inevitable result and obvious symptom is the 'CYB phenomenon'. Translated verbally, this means quite simply, 'cover your back'. Translated into organizational behaviour it means that before doing anything, however minor, everybody will protect himself or herself (particularly in that sensitive area) by making someone else accountable for what is done. We observed widespread CYB in the US Army in Germany, in very refined ways. For example, someone fully authorized to write, sign and send certain categories of letter would only do so after his or her boss had signed the file copy. Since at that time the Army employed some 70 000 civilians in administrative duties, it is fascinating to speculate on the total cost of the various manifestations of CYB.

2. *Is the system used by managers as a weapon to beat their subordinates?*

We know of a UK company in which a certain department head conducts what his subordinates affectionately call his 'weekly blame meeting'. Everybody knows that somebody's head will roll – it always does – but they don't know whose head it is going to be. The subordinates spend each week preparing alternative defences or excuses, in anticipation of the dreaded meeting.

3. *Is the system perceived as a non-threatening source of information, designed to help managers to do their jobs properly by enabling each to measure his or her own performance?*

This is the ideal situation, defined in an article in the *Harvard Business Review* as 'commitment rather than control in the workplace'. It represents the consequence of a team process in making plans and implementing them.

What effect does the control system have?

We believe that the effectiveness of the control system should be judged in terms of two criteria:

- Does it maximise the probability that actual results will conform to the plan?
- Does it result in improved group and individual managerial performance?

OPERATING SYSTEMS

The process of making and selling products or providing services requires the availability of operating systems which supply the data necessary for planning, decision-making, problem-solving and control.

Traditionally, financial records were always the best organized and the most accurate, because of external demands (the law, shareholders, banks, tax authorities, etc), and because of the need to collect and pay monies. It was financial records which were first mechanized and then computerized, to ensure the greatest degree of control. Generally, these included:

- Billing, customer records and credit control
- Sales records and sales analysis
- Financial accounting
- Financial planning and control (especially of cash flow)
- Wages and salary preparation
- Cost accounting.

After financial records, the tendency was to use the computer for administrative applications, in an attempt to save clerical costs.

In manufacturing companies, the records of purchase of materials and components, production planning and control, quality control and preventive maintenance were very often kept by hand, and decisions relating to these areas were left to 'good judgement'. With the growing complexity of operations, it became clear that hand-written records and good judgement would not suffice. This has led to a proliferation of software packages, aimed at the production process itself, particularly relating to:

- Materials and components purchase
- Inventory control
- Production planning and control
- Quality control
- Decision-support systems.

Financial and administrative records still predominate and the planning and control of physical operations is still not widely enough practised. Where computerized operations systems have been introduced, they are frequently inadequate for the real needs of the business and often produce inaccurate data, leading to wrong decisions and inappropriate behaviour.

We hear most complaints about marketing information systems, where marketers feel the lack of comprehensive data in well organized databases, kept up to date and readily accessed. On the other hand, the access to external databases via the company's computer now makes available enormous amounts of market and other data, which it would be impossible to keep internally.

Manufacturing performance cannot be regarded as efficient where excessive inventories are carried (either because of a deliberate 'just-in-case' policy or because of the fallibility of good judgement), where production is stopped by lack of materials or parts (or is continued by the expensive flying-in of missing items), or where output is irregular due to bottlenecks in manufacture or breakdown of equipment.

We strongly recommend that companies which have not yet installed computerized operations systems should investigate the options available. In broad terms, they include the following:

- MRP: Material Requirements Planning
- MRP II: Manufacturing Resource Planning
- OPT: Optimized Production Technology

A few words of explanation will indicate what they provide.

- MRP: This is a simple mathematical tool which breaks products into components and sub-assemblies, and coordinates the ordering and delivery of all components, and the production starting date of all sub-assemblies. It places great emphasis on the timing of these activities.

- MRP II: This is claimed to be a complete management system, which integrates marketing, purchasing, production and financial planning, by defining the resources required for each activity, and comparing these requirements with what is available.

- OPT: This is a software package, based on complex algorithms. It uses factory-floor input to locate bottlenecks (points in the production flow where there are scarce skills; a high rate of machine failure; time-consuming set-up time or operations). It then uses these data to suggest solutions. This system is suitable for plants with production processes involving many steps and thousands of parts.

It has become fashionable to talk about JIT: the 'just in time' method of inventory control. This method simply means postponing the delivery of materials or parts to a facility, to hours or even minutes before they are to be used. It is intended to reduce inventories and warehouse costs, set-up times and lead times, and to improve quality. JIT allows manufacturers to produce small quantities of many different items. It is good for companies which have continuous processing of standard items. JIT does not require software; it is not so much a system as a way of close collaboration with suppliers. For this reason, JIT requires very reliable suppliers and a cooperative rather than a confrontational relationship with them.

The successful implementation of operations systems depends not only on how well they are designed, but on how well they are used. Perhaps the most critical factor is the meticulous accuracy of the data. Some years ago, someone wrote with tongue-in-cheek, 'Reality is whatever is reported to the system.' Since there is a great deal of truth in this statement, every effort has to be made to ensure the accuracy of data as recorded on the factory floor and as introduced into the system.

THE INFORMATION FUNCTION

Since operating systems are becoming more complex and interdependent, it is almost inevitable that they should be computer-based. This development makes companies more dependent on the on-going and effective performance of the information function.

However, in many companies, the information function is a problem area. Significant capital sums are invested in hardware and in purchasing or developing software. Periodically, further large amounts are required for the replacement of equipment and updating software. Operating costs are very high because of the salaries of highly paid systems analysts, programmers and operators. On the other hand, the completion of new software development is frequently delayed, project costs escalate, service levels are not achieved, and labour turnover is excessive. In extreme cases there is passive or active end-user resistance and even sabotage by clerical staff.

Most frustrating of all, operating managers are dissatisfied with the information which they receive, claiming that the information function does not adequately contribute towards achieving company objectives in that it fails to provide the necessary data for:

- Planning
- Decision making
- Problem solving
- Control.

The introduction of new information systems is frequently unsuccessful, not because of technological shortcomings, but because of a poor fit between the system and the organizational environment of the intended users. The problem stems from:

- Lack of comprehensive planning for information resource management
- The position of the information function in the organisation
- The perceptions of the data processing professionals.

These factors can be summarized as the consequence of an 'equipment orientation' rather than a 'users' needs orientation'. In the choice of data-processing equipment, the high capital costs make it necessary to justify the investments by economies of scale and significant savings in administrative costs. The data-processing personnel, quite naturally, are preoccupied with the processing capacity of the equipment and its technical features. In recommending replacement of equipment, they are mainly interested in keeping up with the state of the art, and are therefore somewhat susceptible to the persuasive arguments of vendors.

The information function is usually defined in terms of the equipment which is used to gather, process, store and deliver information, so it is almost inevitably located at head office, whence it provides data to various remote users with whom it has no personal contact. The consequence is that the type and the flow of information is determined by the limitations of the equipment, departmental barriers and the priorities of the data-processing personnel.

We had the opportunity of seeing the consequences of such a situation when we worked with the housing department of the US Army in Germany. Departmental engineers developed budgets for each project separately, estimating each expense items separately, (wages, materials, etc). The budgets, and eventually, reports on actual expenses were sent to a central data processing facility at the Pentagon in Washington, where budget reports were prepared for all current housing construction projects together (not recognizing each project individually), giving totals of all wages, and all materials and other expense items. These reports were of no possible use to the engineers, who tried with hand calculators to break down the total amounts on a project-by-project basis.

The development of personal computers and communication systems which make it possible to move information between locations, and the decrease in equipment costs, have reduced the need for centralized data processing. Information resources can now be located at individual decision centres, in terms of users' needs, provided that they comply with acceptable cost/benefit parameters. On the other hand, these new possibilities of dispersed data processing have created new problems in the non-compatibility of hardware and data elements.

In order to achieve effective performance of the information function in terms of the quality of information provided, and cost-effectiveness in terms of the greatest output for the least cost, it is necessary to conduct long-range planning of information resources. The guiding principle must be that the users define information requirements and determine how the information function will operate. The following objectives must be achieved:

- The integration of data: data from different databases can be combined and processed together.
- The integration of technology: equipment and systems can 'talk' to one another.
- The segmentation of data: the filing of data according to clearly defined subjects to facilitate easy access.
- The subdivision of data: the classification of data into sub-categories, so that users can have direct access to specific and relevant information.
- High value of data bases in terms of:
  — completeness
  — avoidance of duplication
  — accuracy
  — timeliness.

The information function must integrate and synthesize data from multiple sources so as to be able to supply the information needs of individual, identifiable users.

It is strongly recommended that this planning process be carried out systematically and formally to ensure that all aspects are dealt with. The process should include the following stages:

1. *Overall survey*
   The objectives of this survey are to define the nature of the company's business, its organization structure and key personnel, and to identify its present information resources.

2. *Detailed analysis*
   The objective of the analysis is to obtain a thorough understanding of the company, which is the essential requirement for developing an efficient information function. The following information must be obtained:

   - The company's long-term objectives, as defined in its current strategic plan and a projection of its future objectives in the light of its probable directions of growth.
   - The annual operational objectives of each of the divisions and departments.
   - The geographical location of each division and department, the activities of each, their organization structures and reporting relationships.
   - A clear definition of the information requirements of each organizational unit and of individual managers.

3. *Identification of possible data processing applications* ranked according to their potential value to the company.

4. *Identification of possible technical options* for the collection, storage, processing and transmission of data in relation to the applications defined at stage 3 (for example: centralized *v* decentralized facilities, hardware configurations, etc).

5. *Analysis of the technical options defined at stage 4* in terms of:
   - investment required
   - time frame for implementation
   - human resources required
   - operating costs
   - benefits.

   A critical element in assessing technical options is the risk of the business needs outgrowing the system. The following questions should be asked:
   - Can the system handle additional or multiple locations?
   - How large can the system grow in terms of increased function and volume?
   - How difficult or costly will it be to obtain additional capacity without significantly changing the system?

6. *Organizational risk assessment*
   This stage is essential in order to determine the level of risk associated with each technical option and to define the appropriate strategy which will ensure the successful implementation of the selected option.
   The following is a structured guide for examining the conditions which determine organizational risk:

   - Preparedness of senior management.
     This refers in the first instance to the level of involvement and commitment of the senior managers of the user groups to the proposed changes, and to their knowledge and ability to manage the process of change. Many new applications of information technology require little from senior management. For example, managers will probably have a high degree of preparedness for the computerization of existing accounting functions which call for minor organization changes. On the other hand, a programme to reduce the costs of clerical staff by the introduction of new technology, the redesign of all jobs, and the consequent redundancy of many people, will call for a high level of understanding of the technology, and a great deal of time and perseverance in managing the process of change. The level of understanding of the technology will depend on the degree of computer literacy of the managers and on their previous experience in using or introducing computer technology.
     It is also necessary to assess the willingness of these managers to accept training for themselves, and the time and involvement they are prepared to devote to the project.

   - Required speed of implementation.
     This requirement should be considered in relation to managers' past experience in managing change.

   - Potential impact on potential users.
     Two enquiries must be made:
     — an assessment of the receptivity of potential users towards the new technology
     — an analysis of necessary changes in the job environment of the users, by examining the following elements:
       □ the organization structure: if major changes will be necessary to realize the potential benefits of the application, then careful consideration must be given to possible reactions of people who will be affected, particularly if redundancies will be caused, and to developing an appropriate plan for implementation.

☐ the role of the boss: if the new system will be seen as sub-
verting the authority of the users' immediate supervisor, or if
he or she will have to change his or her management style,
again special measures will have to be taken.

☐ jobs and workflow: it is essential to define exactly what
changes will result in the content of people's jobs and the way
in which the work will be organized, and to prepare people
accordingly.

7. *Selection of most desirable options*

Projects with low to moderate organizational risk can be undertaken
immediately. If there is high organizational risk (low managerial
readiness, inability to implement at the necessary pace, unfavourable
receptivity to the new system), then these conditions may have to be
changed, before any attempt can be made to start the project.

8. *Development of plans for the implementation of the chosen options.*

PERFORMANCE EVALUATION

Reams have been written on the subject of the evaluation of managers'
performance, with arguments being offered both in favour and against. The
most important negative aspects are the lack of objective criteria, the possible
bias of the manager making the evaluation, and the defensive behaviour
which will be evoked in the subordinate in the face of criticism. The point is
also made that since the boss and the subordinate are in regular daily contact,
and since the boss will give timely comment to the subordinate as a matter of
course, therefore a periodic formal review is unnecessary.

In a fine paper, entitled 'Performance Appraisal' (March 1988), Graham
James of the Work Research Unit of ACAS (the Advisory Conciliation and
Arbitration Service) has summarized the literature and findings of a 1986
survey by the Institute of Personal Management on performance appraisal.
Essentially, the problems can be set out as follows:

Lack of clarity as to the objectives of performance appraisal.
Where the objectives have not been clearly and unambiguously specified and
have not been understood by all involved, then possible misunderstandings
and dysfunctional behaviour will result. Examples of potentially
incompatible objectives are quoted:

— to let employees know where they stand
— to develop employees in their present jobs
— to develop employees for higher jobs
— to form the basis for individual merit payments.

- Inaccurate assessments because of lack of valid criteria and reliable data. Inaccurate assessments generate feelings of injustice, with negative implications for the culture of the organization.
- Errors in rating, including the following:
  - the *Halo Effect:* an excellent rating on one factor leads the rater to give the employee a similar rating on other factors.
  - the *Leniency/Severity Effect:* a general tendency by the rater to give very high or very low ratings to all employees
  - the *Contrast Effect:* the tendency to assess an employee in comparison with other employees rather than in relation to the requirements of the job.
  - the *Similarity Effect:* the tendency of the rater to rate the employee in relation to him or herself, giving higher ratings to people perceived as similar.
  - the *Error of Central Tendency:* rating all employees in the middle of the scale, that is, always giving a 'safe' rating.
  - the *First Impression Tendency:* the distortion of assessments because of previous impressions gained of the employee.
  - the *Recency Error:* the tendency to give excessive weight to events closer to the date of the appraisal.
  - *Overdependence on a single source of information.*
  - *Stereotyping:* ascribing characteristics to an individual on the basis of group membership. (For example, all redheads are quick tempered.)

While recognizing the validity of the above points, we believe that regular, systematic evaluation of managers' performance is one of the most valuable management systems, since it provides the opportunity for an overall review of a manager's recent performance in relation to his or her job objectives. When using the term 'manager', we are referring to all levels of management, including first-level supervisors. Despite the fact that we have had no direct experience in measuring the performance of non-managerial employees and manual workers, we feel that attempts to do so are desirable, particularly for people doing non-repetitive work.

In Chapter 3 we described managerial standards of performance as acceptable levels of achievement, agreed in advance between the job-holder and the boss, which serve as objective and mutually acceptable criteria for self-measurement and self-control by the job-holder, and as the basis for performance evaluation by the job-holder's boss. We believe that if standards are set in this way, then the evaluation will be seen as fair and relevant by the subordinate. No use should be made of a rating system; the assessment should be strictly in terms of achievement of the predetermined standards.

We believe that performance evaluation should not be done by the personnel department, but only by the boss of the job-holder. The results of the evaluation should be available to the subordinate, and should not be filed in his or her personal record in the personnel department. The evaluation discussion should represent a part of the working relationship between the boss and the subordinate, and be seen by the subordinate as a way of helping him or her to do the job better.

We believe that performance evaluation should primarily be used as a means of improving performance. However, since it is based on objective criteria, it can also serve as the basis for salary review. Unfortunately, in salary review discussions, employees are not likely to be willing to define their shortcomings; they would rather justify their lack of achievement in order to ensure salary increases.

We suggest that performance evaluation discussions take place at least twice a year, once at 'money time' and once when salary changes are not under consideration. Performance evaluation on a quarterly basis would of course be more desirable, thus reinforcing the performance improvement aspect. It would strengthen the relationship between boss and subordinate and preserve the feeling of mutual trust, at the same time achieving greater objectivity in salary review.

The process of conducting managerial performance evaluations is an extremely difficult one, both for the person conducting the evaluation, and for the person being evaluated. This is especially so where the performance of the subordinate has been below the agreed standards.

We believe that the process can be made less inquisitorial and more beneficial if the following points are observed by the person conducting the evaluation:

- Try to conduct evaluations frequently during the year.

- Prepare for the discussion by making a careful comparison of the subordinate's actual performance with his or her predetermined standards.

- Give the subordinate adequate advance notice of the evaluation meeting, so that he or she can make his or her own evaluation.

- Listen more, talk less – in other words, try to get the subordinate to evaluate him or herself.

- Maintain objectivity by assessing results and, if necessary, observed behaviour, but not characteristics or personality.

- Avoid comparisons with others.

- Apply a problem-solving approach: do not blame, but rather try to identify what went wrong; analyse the reasons and try jointly to develop ways of preventing similar errors or shortcomings in the future.

- Preserve the self-esteem of the subordinate.

- Ask, 'How can I help you do your job better?'

There is strong evidence for the validity of this approach. We recall a Swiss company, whose chief executive consistently carried out evaluations of his subordinate managers in this way. These managers regarded the evaluation discussion as a positive and useful experience – almost as a catharsis – and requested that it be done more frequently. At management seminars, when we discuss this topic, we always ask those participants who are living under such a regime if they would prefer to give it up and revert to a less rigorous management life-style in which formal evaluations did not take place. The reply has always been that they would not like to give it up; that the evaluations are useful; that since they were partners in defining the measurement criteria, they know that they are objective and therefore their own career progress does not depend on whether their boss likes them, but on their demonstrated achievements.

In some cases, a form of 'peer review' can be very valuable, particularly when there is a great deal of interaction and mutual interdependence between the managers. In the company described in Chapter 2, which developed and implemented an ambitious strategic plan, there had previously been a system of control whereby the then chief executive met each manager privately, at frequent intervals, to discuss the manager's performance. The system did not produce results, because personal objectives were not clear, and each manager was able to make excuses for delays and errors by blaming others who were not present. At our suggestion, this form of private discussion was discontinued, and a fortnightly review meeting was instituted. All operating managers attend, and the agenda includes a comparison of actual achievements with the objectives for that period. Since the company is engaged in the on-site design, production and assembly of products ordered to specification by customers, it deals with a number of projects in parallel. Each manager is very much dependent on the others for the completion of his or her tasks within time and cost constraints.

The effect of the new review meeting was quite dramatic; instead of being able to offer convenient excuses in private to the boss, managers now had to justify themselves to a meeting of their peers. One manager, who had always been unsuccessful in achieving objectives and, as a consequence, caused considerable delays and difficulties for other managers resigned shortly afterwards, saying that he could not stand the pressure. Despite the obvious success of this method of continual review, we believe that in addition, a private performance evaluation discussion between boss and subordinate should take place in the manner described.

Some years ago, the US General Electric Corporation conducted a wide-ranging study throughout the company to assess the value of managerial performance evaluation. Their conclusions were significant:

- Managerial performance evaluation is valuable, and can contribute to improvement in performance.

- Criticism of inferior performance only produces resentment and defensive behaviour.

- Praise of the subordinate who has achieved inferior results does not produce improvement.

- The only thing which does improve results is new objectives, set jointly by boss and subordinate.

MATCHING MANAGERIAL SYSTEMS TO HUMAN NEEDS

Managerial systems are devised to ensure that the organization achieves its objectives. However, for these systems to be effective, the individuals who operate them must feel that their personal needs are taken into account, so that their efforts on behalf of the organization will give them job satisfaction and a sense of achievement and personal worth.

The following table summarizes what has been presented thus far in this book.

Human needs	Managerial systems
Tell me what you want me to do.	Personal annual job plan
Tell me how well I must do it.	Managerial standards of performance
Let me get on with it.	Job design/Delegation of authority
Tell me how well I am doing.	Performance evaluation
Help me to improve my performance.	Training

Chapter 6

A Workforce that Really Cares

DEFINING AND SHARING MEANINGFUL COMPANY VALUES

The critical factor in achieving company objectives is the commitment and energy of the entire workforce. Investment in new equipment, introduction of new technologies and development of new processes are essential, but they will achieve nothing without the devoted efforts of everybody in the company.

This commitment comes when people feel a strong sense of identification with the company, feel that they belong, are valuable, and are a part of the team. Any attempt to create such a sense of identification must address the question of 'identification with what?' Obviously, people will not identify with products, buildings and equipment. They may, however, identify with what the company is trying to achieve – with what it stands for. This provides the basis for the concept of 'company culture' (one of the current 'buzz' terms), or 'shared values'. Company beliefs, values and norms define personal behaviour, speech and presentation. They provide a focal point for identification so that everybody can proudly say, 'That's what we believe in and that's what we practise.'

IBM is famous for its three defined company values, which date back to the founding of the company:

- Treating employees with respect and dignity.
- Providing the best service possible.
- Performing tasks in a superior manner.

The entire management system of IBM was developed to support these values, resulting in an employee-oriented company with very high performance goals. IBM's top management has often claimed that this unique company culture has been responsible for the firm's enormous success.

The company culture at the Nissan car factory in Sunderland has existed since the opening of the plant and is remarkable in many ways. Essentially, the culture is 'classless': no distinctions are made between 'staff' and 'hourly paid' people; no one clocks in; there is one style of uniform, one canteen and one car park. This 'single-status society' is seen as the major contributing factor to Nissan's success, particularly in productivity, which is more than double that of some rival British plants.

Eaton Corporation's revolutionary programme to revitalize its factory environment was based upon three defined values:

- A commitment to employee participation in decision making.
- Employee involvement in the total job process.
- The development of policies and practices that do not discriminate between blue-collar and white-collar employees.

These are ideas with which everyone can identify. They give a clear focus for the behaviour of all employees, and provide a basis for a working climate in which people feel good about themselves and about their jobs.

Culture problems

Unfortunately in many companies, values have never been defined. Consequently, the culture that has evolved is based on the behaviour patterns of the most senior employees, who believe that theirs is the best and only way. The working climate then becomes unhealthy and negative, characterized by rigid and insular thinking and behaviour, formal rules and procedures. People feel isolated from top management and from each other, and begin to identify more with their own departments than with the company as a whole. They begin to defend their own territory, to be less communicative and cooperative, and to become involved in interdepartmental and interpersonal conflicts. In extreme cases, they become completely alienated, coming to work only to be registered as present but doing the absolute minimum. In the large steel company referred to in Chapter 4, a totally alienated middle-management group had created a semi-secret internal trade union, which published lists of complaints and threats but refused to be identified personally. Despite large posters everywhere in the plant proclaiming 'Quality is our life', uncaring production workers would cut pieces off red-hot ingots to use for boiling their tea.

Mergers and acquisitions can create problems if there is a clash of different corporate cultures; and multinational companies and organizations, which operate in different national cultures, sometimes suffer from corporate culture clash as well. When companies bring in new chief executives or divisional directors from 'outside', they can be hurt by internal warfare. The new chief executive and his staff of 'outsiders' (often recruited from his or her previous employer) comes into conflict with the rest of the organization. A Spanish company brought in a new divisional director – he was not Spanish but spoke the language – who had been responsible to an American company for its entire South American operation. There was no question of his competence, which manifested itself very quickly in improved results. There was, however, the most serious resentment among the senior managers, who claimed that he was insensitive to the 'idiosyncracies of the Spanish culture'.

Culture clash, culture misfit and unhealthy cultures will inevitably have a negative impact on end-results. Avoiding these problems and making culture a positive force requires top managers' constant attention; they must define and create the culture they want, and then continuously monitor it and actively intervene to maintain its existence.

Managing the company culture

In general terms, the characteristics of a positive culture are obvious: values and norms which are supportive of excellence, customer service, teamwork, profitability, honesty and pride in one's work. However, exactly what constitutes the optimum culture in any specific situation may vary considerably. In a small but growing company, important values may be those that tend to encourage rapid growth: risk-taking, entrepreneurialism and innovation. In a mature, slow-growing company, the most important values may relate to cost-consciousness.

In order to 'manage' the company culture in a systematic way it is necessary to carry out a self-audit (Figure 6.1). An effective self-audit should include these steps.

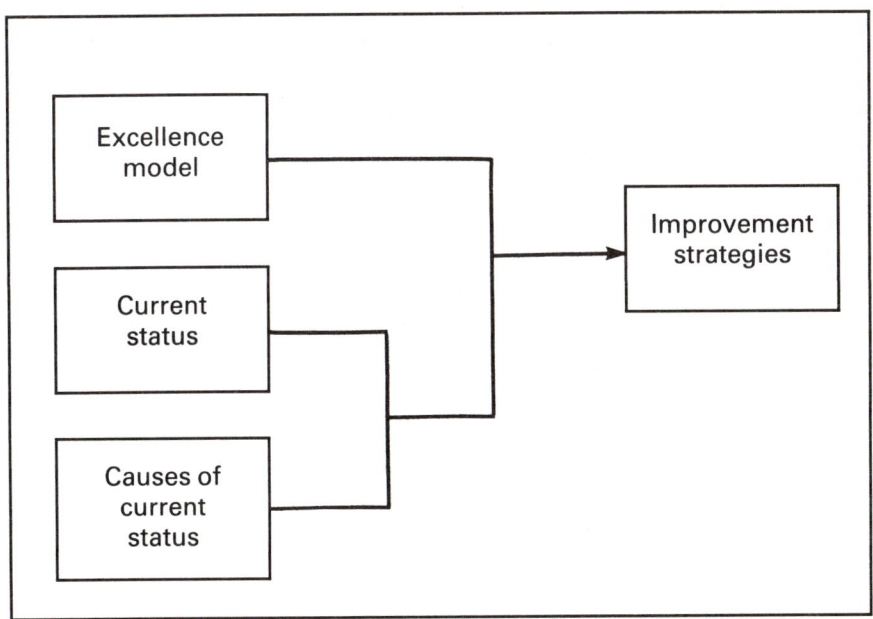

Figure 6.1   *The self-audit process*

1. *Define the culture appropriate for the needs of the company.*

Take into account the nature of the business, its stage of development, long-term and short-term objectives, the strategies for achieving those objectives, and the key factors for success (an excellence model). The parameters to be considered include:

- customer orientation;
- product and service quality;
- profitability;
- quality of the working environment;
- leadership style;
- teamwork and communication;
- personal honesty and integrity;
- change and innovation.

Figure 6.2 shows an interesting example of a 'values statement'. The Penney Idea was adopted in 1913, which goes to show that there is nothing new about the concept of company culture, except perhaps the name. A further example, with a different emphasis, is the statement of the managerial philosophy of the Toyota Auto Body Division (Figure 6.3).

2. *Measure the existing culture, both in general terms and in terms of the desired criteria.*

General analysis aids understanding of the current norms and behaviour in the company and exposes weaknesses. There are three types of organizational culture profile: bureaucratic, innovative and supportive.

- *Bureaucratic cultures* are hierarchical, with clear definition of responsibilities and decision-making authority. The work is well organized and systems are effective. Bureaucratic cultures are usually power-oriented, with very strong managerial controls; and cautious, with a great reverence for tradition. They are most appropriate for companies with a large share in a stable market.

- *Innovative cultures* emphasize change, challenge and risk-taking. They are appropriate for creative, results-oriented work-places where stimulation is constant.

- *Supportive cultures* are characteristic of harmonious working climates, with open, trusting, sociable and encouraging relationships. The J C Penney Company, whose value statement is shown in Figure 6.2, has a very supportive culture and a management style based on the humanistic principles set out in 1913.

Figure 6.4 shows the type of questionnaire that could be used to identify the dominant characteristics of an organization. It should be completed anonymously by everybody in the company, or at least by a representative

The Penney Idea

Adopted 1913

— 1 —

To serve the public, as nearly, as we can, to its complete satisfaction.

— 2 —

To expect for the service we render a fair remuneration and not all the profit the traffic will bear.

— 3 —

To do all in our power to pack the customer's dollar full of value, quality and satisfaction.

— 4 —

To continue to train ourselves and our associates so that the service we give will be more and more intelligently performed.

— 5 —

To improve constantly the human factor in our business.

— 6 —

To reward men and women in our organization through participation in what the business produces.

— 7 —

To test our every policy, method and act in this wise: 'Does it square with what is right and just?'

Figure 6.2 *The Penney Idea – a values statement from 1913*

MANAGERIAL PHILOSOPHY
TOYOTA AUTO BODY
FUJIMATSU PLANT

1. **Trust a man and entrust him with tasks**

2. **Present targets to stimulate creative powers**

3. **Train for leadership to enhance capacity for teamwork**

4. **Keep in close communication**

5. **Grasp the personal attitudes of workers**

6. **Re-affirm company commitment to education and training**

7. **Perform technical skill training**

Figure 6.3 *The Toyota managerial philosophy*

Organizational Culture Index

Please circle a score from the scale below which most closely corresponds with how you see your organization.

0	1	2	3
Does not describe my organization	Describes my organization a little	Describes my organization a fair amount	Describes my organization most of the time

		0	1	2	3
a)	risk-taking	0	1	2	3
b)	collaborative	0	1	2	3
c)	hierarchical	0	1	2	3
d)	procedural	0	1	2	3
e)	relationships-oriented	0	1	2	3
f)	results-oriented	0	1	2	3
g)	creative	0	1	2	3
h)	encouraging	0	1	2	3
i)	sociable	0	1	2	3
j)	structured	0	1	2	3
k)	pressurized	0	1	2	3
l)	ordered	0	1	2	3
m)	stimulating	0	1	2	3
n)	regulated	0	1	2	3
o)	personal freedom	0	1	2	3
p)	equitable	0	1	2	3
q)	safe	0	1	2	3
r)	challenging	0	1	2	3
s)	enterprising	0	1	2	3
t)	established, solid	0	1	2	3
u)	cautious	0	1	2	3
v)	trusting	0	1	2	3
w)	driving	0	1	2	3
x)	power-oriented	0	1	2	3

Scoring: BUREAUCRATIC Profile: Add scores for — d,e,j,l,n,t,u,x
INNOVATIVE Profile: Add scores for — a,f,g,k,m,r,s,w
SUPPORTIVE Profile: Add scores for — b,e,h,i,o,p,q,v

Figure 6.4 *A questionnaire like this can be used to identify a company culture*

number of people from every department and every level.

3.   *Define quite specifically the behaviour required to implement and maintain the desired values.*

This is necessary because of the very real difficulty of translating cultural values at the company level into consistent behaviour at the individual level.
Two examples of defined behaviour are given below.

ACTIONS TO ENSURE HIGH QUALITY PRODUCTS AND SERVICES

All managers must:

1.   Continually reinforce the importance of high quality products and services.
2.   Continually communicate to all employees the importance of their contribution to product/service quality.
3.   Encourage the habit of continuous improvement.
4.   Continually stimulate employees' ideas for quality improvement.
5.   Continually seek customers' ideas for quality improvement.

All employees must:

1.   Have a clear understanding of the identity and requirements of customers.
2.   Have a clear understanding of the customers' perception of acceptable quality.
3.   Be completely familiar with the company's products and services, their performance and their possible applications.
4.   Be familiar with the company's specifications of acceptable quality for products and services.
5.   Be familiar with the company's methods of measuring quality of products and services.
6.   Continually request customers' opinions on the quality of the company's products and services.
7.   Continually identify and minimize any factors which tend to reduce the quality of products and services.
8.   Continually identify and strengthen any factors which tend to improve the quality of products and services.

ACTIONS TO ENSURE EXCELLENCE IN EMPLOYEE COMMUNICATIONS

Top management must:

1. Define clearly and communicate to all employees:
    * organizational values
    * organizational policies
    * long- and short-term objectives
    and ensure that they are understood and accepted.
2. Define clearly and communicate to all employees the organization's expectations regarding:
    * product and service quality
    * managerial behaviour.
3. Inform all employees of the organization's achievements and its financial results.
4. Inform all employees of environmental changes (legal, technological, economic, competitive), which may have a major impact on the organization.
5. Ensure that the process of communication should be both by published statements from top management, and by team briefings at every level in the organization, where managers present and discuss matters with their subordinates.
6. Encourage frequent direct discussion between managers and their subordinates.
7. Ensure that managers at all levels achieve a complete agreement with each of their subordinates on their personal job objectives and responsibilities, and their decision-making powers.
8. Ensure that managers at all levels, conduct periodical performance evaluation discussions with each of their subordinates.
9. Encourage all employees to voice their opinions about the values and policies of the organization and to offer suggestions for improving its operations.
10. Ensure that prompt and serious consideration is given to employees' opinions and recommendations, and that appropriate rewards are given for money saving (or money making) ideas.
11. Ensure that all managers actively encourage their subordinates to express their career and personal aspirations.
12. Ensure that all employees are informed about:
    * job opportunities within the organization
    * the requirements of these jobs in terms of experience, knowledge, skills, attitudes and behaviour.
13. Ensure that all employees receive what they believe is relevant, understandable, timely and truthful information.
14. Continually assess the effectiveness of communication methods.

4. *Identify any discrepancies between the desired and the existing culture.*

Rank the discrepancies so that, if there are many, it will be possible to deal with the most important first.

5. *Plan how to deal with the discrepancies*

6. *Implement the plans.*

7. *Periodically, repeat the whole process.*

The process of inducing behavioural change merits some comment. Frequently it is asked whether people's behaviour can more easily be influenced and modified than their attitudes. The answer is clear: it is easier to introduce new behaviour patterns, which can be described, modelled, copied, practised and monitored (either by observation or in training sessions on video), than it is to modify existing attitudes. However, it seems that once new behaviour has been established, attitudinal change follows.

Effective change embraces the roles and responsibilities of managers and employees, and the relationships between them. Much more autonomy must be given to employees, and supervisors must forgo their traditional 'boss' role and see themselves as facilitators of the work of their teams. Once the structure of the organization has been changed, new behaviour becomes possible.

The responsibility for implementing a new culture through new behaviour lies with four groups of company managers:

Top management has the prime responsibility for defining the desired behaviour patterns and for ensuring that they are introduced and maintained throughout the company. However, the key to successful implementation lies less in the 'big decisions' than in top management's own everyday behaviour towards their subordinates, and the consistency of that behaviour. Top management must require middle managers to adopt a similar behaviour pattern, and they, in turn, direct their first-line supervisors. It may be necessary for top management to set up a reward system.

Middle managers are the key to modifying the behaviour of supervisors, by providing role models, giving the necessary training, and directing the supervisors.

First-line supervisors, who are in direct daily contact with the workforce, have the responsibility of creating the desired work-unit culture. In companies where supervisors have been permitted to develop behavioural styles which are incongruent with top management's values, and therefore detrimental to effective performance, achieving change will require significant effort by middle management.

The personnel department should assess the work-unit cultures, advise top management, and develop programmes to help middle managers in their implementation.

QUALITY OF WORKING LIFE

One of the most important company values, perhaps the greatest potential influence in creating a workforce that really cares, is 'quality of working life'. The term itself was coined in 1972 at an international conference on the theory and practice of the democratization of work. Since then, what began as an academic concept has become the subject of ever-increasing interest among operating managers, who are convinced of its relevance and practical significance. In America, for example, AT&T, General Motors, Alcoa, and other large companies have incorporated QWL principles into their management practices. Firms in Canada, the United Kingdom, continental Europe and Australia have followed suit and achieved significant benefit.

The essential concepts of quality of working life were presented very concisely in September 1983, in an occasional paper by Mansell and Rankin, on behalf of the Ontario Quality of Working Life Centre.

- In order to be efficient, organizations must recognize the following characteristics:
  - Organizations function in a continuous two-way interaction with their environment, and cannot isolate themselves from it. The environment of most organizations is complex, and subject to frequently unpredictable change.
  - Organizations therefore need the capacity for strategic planning to determine appropriate responses to environmental change, and great flexibility so as to be able to change themselves totally.
  - Organizations need a workforce which is competent, adaptable and responsible.

- In order to develop a workforce which will enable the organization to function efficiently, the organization itself must be designed to support the positive characteristics of people:
  - People have the need for, and take pride in achievement.
  - People have the need and the ability to learn continually.
  - People need continual stimulation of their minds and senses.
  - People are naturally social and enjoy mutually supportive relations with others.
  - People are purposeful: for their self-esteem, they need to know that they are making a contribution.
  - People need freedom and autonomy, and are capable of responsible self-regulation.

- Organization and job design should therefore ensure that:
  — Hierarchies are minimal, and artificial barriers do not exist between people or functions.
  — Decisions are made at the lowest possible level, to permit the greatest degree of self-regulation by individual and groups.
  — People do not work on fragmented, meaningless tasks; individuals or integrated groups are responsible for a 'whole' job.
  — People working in production jobs are responsible for quality and quality control.
  — Operating systems promote and support integration and self-regulation. For example, information systems provide immediate feedback directly to those who need the information to perform their jobs; information is not used to retain power or to police others.

Figures 6.5 and 6.6 illustrate the implications of the QWL concept. Figure 6.5 shows the traditional hierarchical form of organization in which a manager, working through one or more management levels, directs and controls individual employees, each performing a fragmented task. Figure 6.6 shows a form of organization structure based on QWL principles. In this case, the organization (or a senior manager) working through an appropriate 'linking function' (and minimal intermediary levels), directs a self-managing (or at least a semi-autonomous) group who have accepted responsibility for a common objective. When a group of workers have accepted responsibility for achieving an objective, they must learn to collaborate in the planning, coordination and control of the separate tasks involved. Ideally, they should also learn the skills required for the various tasks. In certain cases, multi-skilling, or learning each other's job, is not possible or is impractical at the time of formation of the group. A self-managing group can nevertheless be formed, provided the members take responsibility for the effective coordination of their activities as a group.

Not only must the group learn to monitor and control the performance of its members, it must also learn to cope with fluctuations in work-flow requirements and individual work loads. Members must therefore learn to plan for and negotiate their individual contributions. Implicit in this is the need to learn to tolerate their individual differences as people.

Since the self-managing group is part of a larger organization, it is in fact semi-autonomous. The group must therefore learn to manage its relations with other groups in the larger organization.

Self-managing groups need to acquire new skills to enable them to carry out functions which were previously performed by supervisors:

- Managerial skills
  — The ability to plan and monitor their activities, to use statistical quality control techniques, and to understand sophisticated

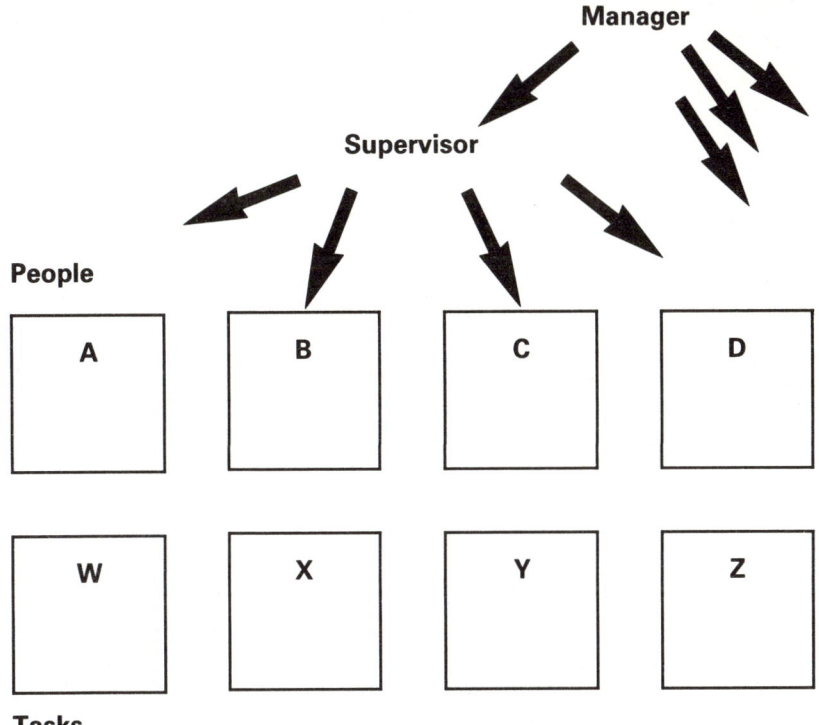

Figure 6.5 *A traditional, hierarchical organization*

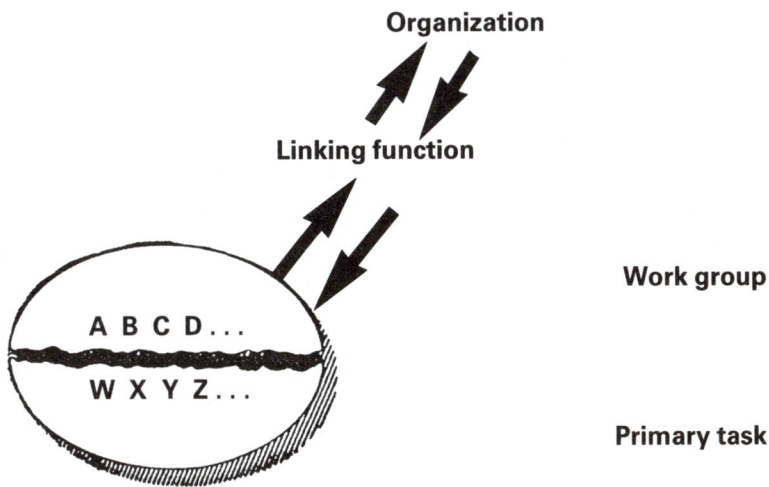

Figure 6.6 *An organization structured on quality of working life principles*

71

management information systems.
  — The ability to solve problems and to take decisions in a systematic
    and rational way.

- Job design skills
  — The ability to analyse tasks and work elements and to combine them
    into acceptable job definitions

- Communication skills

- Skills for creating and maintaining a productive climate.

Acquiring these skills is not easy, particularly for people who have been
accustomed to following orders, and to working in an autocratically managed
organization. Acquiring them, however, provides the opportunity for
considerable personal growth and satisfaction.

QUALITY, SERVICE AND PRODUCTIVITY: A WAY OF LIFE

One corporate value which should be clearly defined and continuously
preached and reinforced is commitment to quality, service and productivity,
in all aspects of the company's activities. A competitive company must
provide exactly the goods and services that the customer requires, at a level
of quality which the customer perceives as appropriate (fitness for purpose),
at a price which the customer perceives as reasonable (value for money),
and at a cost which is profitable to the company. This means not only
commitment, but a never-ending effort to improve the levels achieved.

Changing attitudes to quality

For many years the entire focus on management attention in manufacturing
plants was on maximizing output. Quality of the product was assured by
inspecting raw materials, components and sub-assemblies during production,
and then the final products. Those items which did not conform to
predetermined standards were rejected and thrown away as scrap, or sent
back for reworking. This approach seemed to be correct while western
industry dominated the world and mass-produced items could be sold
everywhere. Product quality was not seen as important, quality-related costs
were not known, and high quality was viewed as a cause of increased costs and
as preventing high productivity.

The impact of competition from Japan and other countries in the Far East
has forced western manufacturers to re-examine their traditional practices
and analyse the reasons for the success of Asian companies. A particularly
dramatic example of the differences between American and Japanese industry

was given in 1983 in the report on a comparative study carried out by Professor David Garvin of the Harvard Business School. He compared the defect rate of US and Japanese home air-conditioners by measuring assembly-line defects per 100 units and service calls per 100 units under the first-year warranty cover. The results were clear: the worst Japanese air-conditioner had a failure rate of less than half that of the best American one. During the production process American firms had 63.5 defects per 100 units, whereas the Japanese had 0.95. In the first year of use, American firms received 10.5 service calls per 100 units, whereas the Japanese received only 0.6. The report, which was entitled *Quality on the Line*, described its findings as 'a shocking indictment of American mediocrity'.

During recent years attitudes have changed significantly in all western countries, as is indicated in this statement by the chairman of Corning Glass Works, quoted in the 1987 *Fortune* magazine report on quality: 'With the current emphasis on competitiveness and the realities of a changing global market-place, no one will survive without a commitment to quality.'

In 1987, The Gallup Organization Inc, on behalf of The American Society for Quality Control, conducted a survey on executives' perceptions of the quality of American products and services. The 615 interviews yielded a number of important findings:

1.   70 per cent ranked internal management (ie improving productivity and quality, educating and training employees) as the most important means of strengthening American ability to compete internationally in business.

2.   80 per cent believed that quality plays a very important role in the ability of American business to compete internationally.

3.   Service quality, product quality and productivity were most frequently rated as the critical issues facing any company.

4.   46 per cent of executives stated that through quality improvement they had achieved a significant increase in market share and profitability.

5.   Concerning the relationship between quality, profit and costs, the majority of executives stated that increasing quality leads to greater profits, whereas 43 per cent stated that increasing quality leads to cost reduction.

6.   The following responses indicate how many executives voted as 'very important' each of these eight methods of improving quality:

	%
• employee motivation	85
• change in corporate culture	82
• employee education	74
• process control	53
• expenditure on capital equipment	45
• more control over suppliers	36
• more inspection	29
• improved administrative support	28

7.   44 per cent of respondents believed that the cost of poor quality is equivalent to 5 per cent of gross sales, whereas 19 per cent believed that it is equivalent to 5–10 per cent of revenues. This is a very surprising finding, since studies in America have indicated that usually the costs of poor quality are equivalent to 20 per cent of revenues.

8.   The cost-ranking of items associated with quality was as follows (the total exceeds 100 per cent owing to multiple responses):

	%
• lost sales	36
• rework costs	23
• repair costs	12
• scrap costs	10
• warranty costs	7
• inspection costs	5
• don't know	10

9.   Frequency of use of various quality-control programmes is shown by the following list. Respondents stated which methods were used 'very often' and 'often'.

	%
• visible top-management leadership	81
• employee involvement in problem-solving	71
• total quality control	63
• evaluation of quality objectives as part of personnel evaluation	59
• mandatory skills training	58
• statistical process control	45
• internal and external surveys	41
• quality improvement teams – salaried personnel	39
• quality improvement teams – hourly personnel	38

10.   Cost-cutting measures with the greatest potential were ranked as follows (the total exceeds 100 per cent owing to multiple responses):

	%
• increase in level of employee motivation	37
• automation or other process improvement	25
• advances in technology	25
• upgrading employees' education/training	25
• making improvements in quality	24
• making improvements in operating systems	23
• making improvements in product design	14
• increases in employee remuneration packages	6
• don't know	2

The following conclusions can be drawn:

- There was widespread recognition of the importance of quality, and a belief that better management and a change of corporate culture are necessary to improve quality.
- However, there seems to be a lack of awareness of the true costs of poor quality, and inadequate use of rigorous methods of statistical process and quality control.

Six 'keys' to quality

The 1987 *Fortune* magazine report on quality suggested six 'keys' to 'making quality a way of life'.

1. *Management must be involved, not just committed.*

This means that top management must not only make statements regarding the importance of quality, but must be prepared to take the initiative by:

- Including specific quality and productivity objectives in the corporate strategic plan, and insisting that these objectives are reflected in the operating plans of the various divisions and departments.
- Reorganizing the whole structure of the company, if need be, to achieve better planning and control, and a more effective response to changing market needs.
- Challenging all aspects of 'conventional wisdom' in the company – the traditional beliefs and practices – in order to be as efficient and competitive as the market demands.
- Providing training in quality awareness and basic quality-control techniques to every employee.
- Insisting on the introduction of rigorous quality-control methods in all departments, with particular emphasis on statistical process control.
- Providing on-going support for achieving and maintaining the desired corporate culture.

2. *The customer is king.*

This raises a number of very important and practical ideas:

- Quality should be defined by the customer.
- The company should focus its attention on understanding customers' needs and expectations.
- The company should strive, not just to satisfy customer needs and expectations, but actually to 'delight' the customer.

This concept is presented very succinctly by Peter Drucker in his book, *Innovation and Entrepreneurship*. He says, 'Quality in a product or service is not what the supplier puts in. It is what the customer gets out and is willing to pay for. A product is not quality because it is hard to make and costs a lot of money. This is incompetence. Customers pay only for what is of use to them and gives them value. Nothing else constitutes quality.'

3.   *Pay attention to how quality is delivered.*

Service quality is as important as product quality but is more difficult to define and control, since services are intangible. They cannot be measured, tested or verified in advance of sales; they have a high labour content and reflect the attitudes and behaviour of the provider; the consumption of many services takes place simultaneously with their production (for example, getting a haircut); and they are 'perishable' and therefore cannot be put into stock (an hotel-night booking cannot be sold the next day; the opportunity has been lost for ever).

The quality of services is measured by the difference between the expectation of the customer on the one hand, and the customer's perceived level of service delivery on the other. The gap between them represents the degree of inadequacy – the size of the service problem.

In order to ensure the provision of appropriate services at an acceptable level, it is necessary to identify the significant factors of service demand. A life-insurance company found that customers expected reliability, responsiveness, assurance and empathy, and tangibles in the form of local facilities and the smart appearance of personnel. A bank found that its customers wanted quick, accurate and responsive service. These companies have developed survey instruments that can quantify service performance. A large real-estate firm found that it had to provide its clients with 'value added' services that went beyond traditional brokerage.

4.   *Get employees involved.*

Improving quality and productivity requires an improved problem-solving capacity, a commitment to the idea of continuous improvement (the Japanese have a word for it – 'kaisen'), and the involvement of workers. Inspection processes are not enough; quality must be built into a product during its maufacture. It is therefore necessary that workers should be able to monitor their results, identify non-standard conditions, and stop the production process if they believe that its output is faulty. The elements in this new culture – employee participation, teamwork, commitment, problem-solving groups, tolerance for new ideas, sharing information – amount to a fundamental change in our concepts of managing people.

The success of a Danish multinational cleaning and security services company (employing 80 000 people worldwide) is based on their creation of a 'service culture', and on their never-ending efforts to develop a workforce with a tremendous sense of personal worth.

5.   *Demand perfection from your suppliers.*

There is a growing appreciation of the fact that quality cannot be improved and then maintained unless suppliers are involved. This has led to rigorous programmes of 'supplier accreditation', whereby firms which buy in raw materials, components and sub-assemblies continuously monitor their suppliers' technology, product quality and reliability, delivery, engineering service, and the consistency with which they achieve agreed standards. Failure to maintain such standards means that the supplier loses its accredited status.

6.   *Use quality-control technology.*

It is necessary to introduce rigorous methods of statistical quality control, and to train workers in these methods so that they will be able to measure and analyse the processes which they operate.

It is also necessary to create an awareness of the costs of quality, or perhaps the costs of 'non-quality':

- *Failure* to achieve quality, that is, failure to 'get it right the first time' results in scrap (waste) reworking, and warranty claims.

  The most extreme case of 'not getting it right the first time' we have heard of is that of a Norwegian company, which built a huge platform for an offshore oil rig. The completed platform, as large as a football field, was floated out to the site and slowly submerged to lock on to legs built previously on the seabed. Unfortunately, the slots underneath the platform did not match the legs by one or two centimetres, and it was impossible to complete the construction.

- *Appraisal* – measuring quality – means costs of inspection, testing, etc.
- *Prevention* costs are those for any activities to investigate, prevent or reduce defects and failures.

All these costs are significant. First, they are large. In 1978, according to the Department of Trade and Industry, they were estimated to have been £10 000 million in the UK. Second, the greater part of these costs arises from failure and appraisal. These costs are avoidable; they add nothing to the value of the end-product, but they do increase the price to the customer. Lastly, these costs are generally not measured and are therefore not known. It is essential that quality costs are continuously measured and controlled. The aim should be twofold:

- to reduce the total cost of quality
- within the overall total, to minimize the proportion of failure and appraisal costs and to maximize the proportion of prevention costs.

The concept of total quality

In its 1988 National Quality Campaign report, *Fortune* magazine suggested that it is no longer sufficient to achieve customer satisfaction, what is required is building customer loyalty. In order to do this they suggest six strategies, which to a degree repeat the 'keys' suggested in their 1987 report, but nevertheless do represent a significant and positive approach:

1. Become a partner with your customer.
2. Involve your workers in your business.
3. Work closely with your suppliers.
4. Measure customer satisfaction.
5. Innovate, innovate and reinnovate.
6. Compete on the basis of continuous improvement.

Whereas quality control originated as a technique for the improvement of manufacturing processes, the concept has now been extended to include all aspects of an organization's activities, and the appropriate term, 'total quality', is now widely used. To give an indication of the breadth of this new concept, we quote in full an article written by the senior consultant for corporate quality, at the Productivity and Quality Center, Westinghouse, Pittsburgh, USA.

Responsibilities of the total quality manager

The total quality manager should improve management leadership by:

- Instilling a never-ending quality-improvement process that involves all functions, promotes total quality awareness, and entrenches a solid quality culture that cannot be derailed by short-term pressures.

- Establishing, promoting and participating in (but not necessarily leading) a quality council that involves the entire top-management team in directing the quality-improvement effort.

- Facilitating the development of the organization's long-term strategy and objectives.

- Helping establish yearly quality-improvement objectives for every function, and encouraging their inclusion in each employee's personal goals.

- Helping establish and monitor quality-improvement projects, as well as multifunctional teams to undertake these projects.

- Continually communicating the total quality-improvement process and its successes.

- Providing quality visibility by collecting and analysing performance data, and reporting trends.

The total quality manager should improve customer orientation by:

- Helping develop, display and encourage the use of measures of external customer satisfaction.

- Meeting with external customers to better understand their perceptions, and instigate necessary improvements.

- Promoting the 'internal customer' concept.

- Ensuring the establishment of appropriate controls and improvement efforts for all functions that directly interface with the customer.

The total quality manager should improve product/process leadership by:

- Ensuring the establishment and maintenance of an organization-wide, prevention-oriented quality program plan.

- Participating in developing a comprehensive hardware-design assurance program.

- Encouraging the integration of product and process design, with emphasis on error-free processes.

- Ensuring that adequate control systems are in place to properly set and meet product and process requirements.

- Establishing and coordinating a participative and impartial internal audit program.

- Establishing systems that detect and correct process errors rather than product defects.

- Being knowledgeable of and promoting the use of statistical techniques in all functions.

- Encouraging the use of advanced technology wherever it improves total quality.

- Helping develop programs to measure and improve the accuracy, time-liness [speed] and completeness of the flow of information throughout the organization.

- Developing a wide-ranging external-supplier quality-improvement program.

- Promoting the 'internal supplier' concept.

The total quality manager should improve human resource excellence by:

- Encouraging the concept of personal and departmental responsibility for quality.

- Fostering a participative management climate throughout the organization.

- Helping develop and teach quality awareness and quality-skills training programs for all personnel.

- Participating in identifying functional training needs, and reviewing and contributing to training content and methods.

- Encouraging regular organization analysis and employee surveys to provide a basis for workforce planning and improvement.

- Helping motivate individuals and teams through establishing programs to foster creativity and recognize success.

MAXIMIZING MANAGERIAL PRODUCTIVITY

A most important contributory factor towards developing a workforce that really cares is a management team which is not only highly productive, but is perceived to be so by all employees in the organization. Thus every manager has a double obligation: to be as productive as possible and also to be a positive role model to his or her subordinates.

Managers should be judged by three criteria:

- Are they doing the right things?

- Are they doing them in the shortest time and with the least effort and cost?

- Are they producing the necessary impact and achieving planned results?

Successful performance in terms of all three should be defined as 'productive'.

Many people are preoccupied with being busy, or with appearing to be busy. 'Busy-ness' does not mean 'productivity', since it is very easy to be busy with irrelevant and unimportant activities and to carry them out in a very competent way, using a minimum of time and effort. Finally, it is possible to perform the correct activities, but in such a way as to produce insignificant results.

In recent years, there has been a growth of interest in time management, both in management literature and seminars. As we perceive it, the emphasis of time management is on saving time by, for example, only picking up a piece of paper once, or by conducting meetings more effectively. We believe that the real problem is identifying and concentrating on the 'right things'. Referring back to the examples quoted, why does that piece of paper find its way to the manager's desk at all, and perhaps that meeting should never have been called in the first place?

We recommend that managers analyse their activities in two ways, which should give them valuable insights into the reasons for their unproductive busy-ness, and suggest directions for improvement:

1. *A classification of activities into the following categories:*

- *Value-added work*
  There is no common definition of value-added work. It refers to those activities which are critical to the successful performance of the department; activities which have a significant impact on the achievement of results; activities which contribute most to the completion of projects. The specific definition will be different for each manager, so that each one has a clear understanding, either by rigorous self-analysis, or by discussion with peers and subordinates.

- *Necessary work*
  Activities which must be carried out, but which cannot be classified as value-added (report writing would be a typical example).

- *Rework*
  This classification refers to any activity which has to be done a second time (for example, redrafting a letter; re-negotiating a contract; repeating calculations because of errors).

- *Unnecessary work*
  Any activities which do not contribute anything, but are performed because of tradition or inertia (for example, attending meetings out of fear of insulting the initiator, even though the meeting is irrelevant to the attending manager. When we worked with the US Army, a frequent complaint was the obligation to attend receptions for visiting dignitaries, even though the role of the people attending was purely 'decorative').

- *Non-work*
  This means exactly that; it may mean sitting round the office discussing golf (voluntary idleness), or travelling time (involuntary idleness).

Having classified their activities into these categories, managers should examine ways which will enable them to allocate time, energy and resources to value-added activities, and to minimize their own personal involvement in other types of activity.

2. *Allocation of time between:*

- *Discretionary time*
  This refers to time when the manager does what he or she wants, according to personal choice (performing any of the categories of work indicated above).

- *Non-discretionary time*
  This refers to time spent on activities which were imposed on the manager by other people or by other factors:
  — the boss (who may not always be right, but is always the boss)
  — subordinates (who are expert at 'delegating their problems upwards')
  — the 'system' (for example, preparing weekly expense reports)
  — other factors (for example, incoming telephone calls).

This analysis of time spent can best be done by means of a time log, completed diligently every day for about two or three weeks (Figure 6.7). The findings are usually a revelation: managers suddenly realize that they do not manage, but in fact are 'managed' by others. At the risk of appearing non-democratic or anti open-door policy, we really believe that managers should do their utmost to minimize their non-discretionary time, in order to maximize their discretionary time. Only in this way can they concentrate their efforts on what is really value-added work.

TRAINING

We have included training in this chapter, since we believe that an organization's willingness to provide training is a sign of sincere concern for both the long-term benefit of the organization, and the job security and the career advancement of employees. Training will not only improve the organization's ability to perform, but will contribute to improving the working climate and the workforce's closer identification with the organization.

A worrying report on training in the United Kingdom, entitled, 'A Challenge to Complacency – Changing Attitudes to Training', was prepared in 1985 for the Manpower Services Commission and the National Economic Development Office. The main conclusions of the report were as follows:

- Britain's future international competitiveness and economic performance will be significantly influenced by the speed with which substantial improvements can be made in the scale and effectiveness of training by British companies.

- Most employers do not see training as an issue of major importance.

- Most companies believe that Britain undertrains, compared with its main overseas competitors, but nevertheless think that the amount of training they themselves undertake is about right. The authors of the study felt that this lack of concern reflects complacency.

Name _____

Date _____

Hour	Non-discretionary time				Discretionary time		Activity description	Action to take
	Boss	Subord	System	Other	Used	Waste		
8.30								
9.00								
9.30								
10.00								
10.30								
11.00								
11.30								
12.00								
12.30								
13.00								
13.30								
14.00								
14.30								
15.00								
15.30								
16.00								
16.30								
17.00								
17.30								
18.00								
Total								
%								

Action
A. Continue doing
B. Do differently
C. Delegate
D. Stop doing

Source: D J Jacobs & Associates

Figure 6.7 *Daily time-log*

- This complacency is reinforced by widespread ignorance among top management of how their companies' training activities compare with those of their competitors, both in the UK and overseas.

- The generally low level of importance attached to training was evidenced by the following:
  — decisions on training are delegated to line managers, who often have short-term horizons when considering returns on investment
  — training is rarely seen as an investment, but as an overhead cost which should be cut when profits fall
  — no analysis of training needs or evaluation of training is made
  — training managers have a very low status.

- Training is not seen as an important contributor to competitiveness and profitability. Most believe that high profits lead to increased training expenditure.

- The reluctance to invest in training is reinforced by uncertainties about the future.

- In continental Europe, the USA and Japan, there is a strong driving force for training, either from cultural pressure, or clear legislation.

- Britain's performance on training will only be improved by a major change in employer attitudes to training.

The report recommended three main directions for dealing with the situation:

- Exhorting and encouraging companies to invest in training.

- Harnessing the interests of individuals as a means of bringing pressure to bear on employers.

- Improving the operation of the training market to make it easier for companies to define, and obtain from external providers, the training they require.

Defining training needs

Attempts at defining needs are often a little less than systematic, as evidenced by the following statements by training managers:

- 'Look at all the big companies who use this programme. It's got to be right for us!'

- 'Here are some new subjects that many big firms are starting to include in their programmes. We should too.'

- 'We researched dozens of management programmes. These are the subjects that are common to most of them.'

- 'We're going to get Professors A and B to do our programme. Everybody's talking about how good they are.'

- 'Our programme includes all the things that textbooks say managers should do.'

- 'We asked senior management to give us a list of the subjects they felt should be in the programme. About a third responded, and we've included everything they suggested.'

- 'We sat down and thought of all the things our managers should do better.'

- 'The more we thought about it, the more sure we became that we don't need a programme designed especially for us. Let's use one of the institutional programmes.'

Even in cases where training needs analysis is done more systematically, mistakes are made:

- *The snapshot*
  Needs are analysed once and are not reviewed periodically. Assuming that a company's needs are static may result in training that emphasizes outdated skills.

- *Reactionary responses*
  Training programmes are based on a reaction to a specific one-time set of circumstances, so that there is no long-term benefit to the organization.

- *Biased analyses*
  Selection of topics is based on the trainer's strengths or personal areas of interest. This obviously is of no real value to the organization.

Systematic training needs analysis

A systematic needs analysis must distinguish between:

- Training subjects: skills, relationships, climate

- Training classification: managers, supervisors, workforce
- Individuals
- Organizations: healthy organizations and problem organizations require different diagnostic processes.

The following steps are recommended:

1. Collect information about the organization in order to match training content with critical business issues.

   - *Objectives*
     Long- and short-term objectives
     Time frame
     Priorities.

   - *Changes – assess impact of:*
     — Planned merger or reorganization
     — Introduction of new products and services
     — Opening of new markets
     — Introduction of new technology or of office automation.

   - *External factors – assess impact of:*
     — new government regulations
     — intensified competition.

   - *Performance gaps*
     — Identify performance issues that prevent the work unit or the entire organization from achieving its objectives.

Methods of data collection

Data collection technique	Strength	Weakness
Review of business data	Provides objective data	May take a long time
Personal interviews	Provide in-depth information	Time consuming
Focus groups	Provide overall perceptions	Possible undue influence of informal leader
Informal discussions	Provide direction for further study	Unsystematic

Data collection technique	Strength	Weakness
Questionnaires	Narrow direction for further investigation	Do not provide in-depth information
Observation	Provides first-hand data	Time consuming
Review of performance data	Defines criteria	Possible influence of other factors
Review of job requirements	Provides objective data	Time consuming

2. Identify potential training opportunities.
    Analyse the issues identified in step 1, in order to separate those caused by a lack of knowledge or skills from those caused by other factors.

3. Determine the possible impact of training on those issues which were identified at step 2, and select those where the impact will be greatest.

4. Define the knowledge, skills, behaviour patterns and attitudes which appear to be relevant to the selected issues.

5. Develop appropriate training programmes.

6. Present these programmes.

7. Evaluate the outcome of the programmes.

8. Regularly review training needs in the light of changing circumstances.

Evaluation of training

Trainers tend to use 'body counts' as a measure of their success; that is, the number of courses completed, and the number of students trained. Such an approach is obviously unsatisfactory, since it makes no attempt to measure the impact of the training given.

The following are possible alternative methods for evaluating training.

● *Assessing participants' reactions to a programme.*
    This is unsatisfactory, since participants may report what they believe the trainer wants to hear. Furthermore, courses cannot be judged by whether participants liked them.

- *Collecting anecdotes, incidents and testimonials.*
  This is also unsatisfactory, since there is no obvious link to performance objectives.

- *Measurement of knowledge gains.*
  This can be done in a rigorous way. However, it is incomplete, since improved performance requires behavioural change. Often people know a great deal about a subject, without being able to use it effectively.

- *Measurement of behavioural change.*
  This is most relevant, and can be done by observation, questionnaires, and by reports on participants' behaviour by their bosses, peers and subordinates.

- *Measurement of performance.*
  Departmental or work-unit performance can be measured objectively. However, the performance of a department cannot always be linked directly to the behaviour of the manager, so that it may not be a completely accurate measure of his or her success.

Individual management training needs

At the same time as an overall needs analysis is being made, it is appropriate to define the training needs of the individual manager, in the light of the evaluation of his or her performance and in relation to new objectives for improved performance. In this situation, it is possible for the manager's boss to discusss his or her training needs in a very practical way, and for them jointly to develop a tailor-made training programme which will include clear training objectives in terms of knowledge, skills, attitudes and behaviour patterns, and a time frame for its completion. We suggest that the contents of such a training programme should include the following elements:

Essential managerial knowledge

- Specialist technical knowledge, which is necessary to maintain status in the department.

- A good understanding of the world outside, as the basis for stategic thinking.

- Mathematics and computing as the basis for improved decision-making.

- Human behaviour as the basis for people-management skills.

Essential managerial skills

- Strategic and operational planning, with particular emphasis on the ability to conduct a team planning process, set objectives, and to develop action plans and control systems.

- Organizational planning, with particular emphasis on job design, role clarification (based on personal job objectives), and on effective delegation.

- Performance evaluation
  — The ability to conduct objective evaluations, so as to preserve the self-esteem of subordinates, while helping them to define personal objectives for improvement.

- People-management skills
  — Managing change, particularly the introduction of new technology.
  — Team-building, as the essential basis for effective group work.
  — Interpersonal skills, as the prerequisite for effective management.

Managerial attitudes

- Competitiveness, not on an interpersonal basis, which becomes destructive, but in relation to other companies.

- Respect for other people, even if their views and social status are different.

Managerial behaviour patterns

- Pro-active, as opposed to reactive thinking.

- Continuous challenge to conventional wisdom and tradition; always asking, 'Maybe there is a better way?'

- A participative management style.

- Openness and trust in interpersonal relationships.

- Adult-to-adult behaviour in dealings with other people; that is, protecting the dignity of every individual and recognizing his or her ability to think and make a valuable contribution.

Training of supervisors

Whereas many of the subjects in management training are relevant to first-level supervisors, there are certain topics which are of particular importance to them. The journal, *Training and Development,* reported on a survey in the USA of the opinions of training directors, responsible for supervisory training. The majority identified the following points as critical, and ranked them in the following order of importance:

- Improving productivity
- Handling performance problems
- Problem-solving
- Decision-making
- Giving feedback
- Resolving conflict
- Assigning work
- On-the-job training.

We feel, however, that this list does not encompass all the training needs of supervisors, particularly those who are newly appointed. We would recommend the inclusion of the following:

- Fundamental skills in managing people
- Fundamental skills in communicating with people
- Operational planning and control
- Statistical quality control
- Getting workers' commitment to plans
- Dealing with workers' response to controls
- Giving orders and instructions
- Delegating effectively
- Improving workers' work habits
- Coaching for improved performance
- Dealing with workers' complaints
- Assessing workers' performance
- Using discipline in a positive way
- Dismissing a worker
- Implementing change
- Trade union relations
- Health and safety in the workplace.

Worker training

The nature of work, both in industry and services, is changing very rapidly; the essential trends are an increase in the use of technology; ever-increasing complexity of equipment and processes; a shift away from menial to mental and knowledge work; an increasing tendency to involve workers in the control of the quality of the products which they make, and in the planning and control of their own activities.

Training should be provided which will enable workers to cope with change, and to perform effectively in the new work environment.

TEAM BUILDING

When a group of people is trying to achieve something, (for example, a football team trying to win a match or a manufacturing company trying to achieve a certain level of profit), individuals have to learn to behave as members of a team, each consciously striving for the benefit of the group as a whole.

Team building is one of the most important activities of managers at all levels in an organization. It seeks to create in each subordinate a feeling of identification with others and commitment to achieving group objectives. It also seeks to reinforce each subordinate's feeling that he or she is valuable to the company. Each unit-based, team-building activity should also be seen as part of a company-wide effort to develop and strengthen a sense of identification with the company as a whole. This is the essence of the concept of corporate culture, discussed earlier.

The chief executive should develop a sense of team spirit with his or her senior managers, who should promote a better working climate among their subordinate managers; they, in turn, should concentrate on building effective teams with their own people.

The effective team

The effectiveness of a team can be assessed in terms of these criteria:

- *Team output* The first measure of effectiveness must be the extent to which the team achieves its objectives.

- *Commitment* to the achievement of objectives will be reflected in the team's efforts to succeed, and in the way in which team members help each other.

- *Morale* is indicated by the team's self-image, its optimism and its belief in its ability to overcome difficulties and succeed.

- *Quality of decisions* Team decisions are generally better than unilateral decisions because more aspects of the issue and more possible solutions are considered.

- *Non-distortion of information* Inaccurate information and defective communication are typical of groups which do not function well as teams, and in which individual ambitions are predominant.

91

- *Responsiveness to challenge and change* Effective teams respond enthusiastically to challenge, and provide support to individual team members in dealing with new situations.
- *Creativity* The self-assurance and mutual-support system of an effective team reduce the need to follow conventional wisdom, and thus enable more creative and unconventional approaches to problem solving.
- *Personal development* is encouraged in effective teams, and opportunities provided.

The behaviour of effective teams is characterized as follows:

- A cohesive bond exists between individual team members and the team as a whole.
- A climate of mutual respect and trust enables team members to communicate openly and frankly.
- There is a strong commitment to the achievement of team objectives.
- All members of the team participate actively in the planning process. As a result, they have a sense of 'ownership' of the team objectives and are able to clarify their individual roles in terms of personal job objectives. This enables each person to develop a personal annual job plan, which provides a basis for personal planning and control and also for periodic performance evaluation by the team member's boss.
- All members of the team participate actively in the problem-solving and decision-making process. When a decision has been taken, team members feel committed to its successful implementation.
- Team members listen to one another. They are skilled in giving opinions and advice and receiving constructive feedback.
- Team members are capable of being cooperative and competitive, as appropriate.
- Team members recognize that both they, as individuals, and the team leader have roles to play in building and maintaining team spirit.
- Team members are capable of periodically evaluating their own effectiveness as a team and of taking the necessary corrective action.

The requirements for an effective team can be defined as follows. They must be regarded as a series of building blocks, resting one on another, in the sequence presented here:

- *Mutual respect and trust* are essential; without them, any team-building effort will be defeated. In the absence of mutual trust, cynicism and alienation will prevail, preventing any real discussion of issues.

- *Open communication* which is possible only in a climate of mutual trust, permits candid examination of any issues which may prevent the group from functioning as an effective team.

- *Shared goals*, rather than personal goals, must be the focus for all the efforts of the team members.

- *Systems and procedures* for routine functions must represent an agreement between team members on the best way to act. In many organizations, systems and procedures are defined by some higher authority and are seen as the framework in which a team will develop. This never succeeds.

The team-building process

Team building requires an understanding of human needs and of how the work-place can influence people by fulfilling, or failing to fulfil, those needs. It requires empathy: the ability and willingness to understand other people's feelings. It calls for an awareness of one's own credibility in the eyes of others, and of the impact of one's own behaviour on the working climate. It requires constant attention to building and maintaining trust between group members.

The process of team building should include the following steps, each of which should be carried out by the manager and all the members of his or her team.

1. *Discussion of the validity of a series of assumptions about people at work.*

- As individuals:
    - In general, people wish to work in a challenging environment which provides the opportunity for personal achievement and growth.
    - In general, people both desire and are able to contribute more to the achievement of organizational objectives than the organization permits.

- As members of working groups:
    - The working group represents the most relevant group for most people, from a psychological point of view.
    - In general, people wish to be accepted by members of the working group and to interact cooperatively with them.
    - Suppressed negative feelings and unresolved conflict adversely affect problem solving, personal growth and job satisfaction.
    - In general, people are capable of solving work-related problems.
    - When members of a working group are involved in making decisions, they are more committed to achieving the group objectives.

— Groups of people who really care achieve high levels of productivity and quality.

2.   *Discussion of the characteristics of effective teams,* and an assessment by the group of the extent to which it perceives itself as effective.

3.   *Identification of the issues which prevent the team from functioning effectively.*

4.   *Feedback by each person to other members of the team,* describing those aspects of their behaviour at work which help others to function well, and those which hinder. This process must be very carefully controlled so that it does not degenerate into mutual criticism but remains as factual and non-threatening as possible.

5.   *Development of action plans for problem solving:*

● Dealing with the issues which prevent the team from functioning effectively.

● Making necessary behavioural changes.

6.   *Disclosure by each person of his or her personal motivations and job-satisfaction needs.* One person may value personal security, another may be looking for more challenge. Discuss ways of redesigning people's jobs so that they can achieve a higher degree of job satisfaction.

We have found, in conducting workshops on team building, that this process allows people to talk about various aspects of team effectiveness in an impersonal way, and subsequently to begin to disclose their own personal feelings about the same issues.

IMPROVING MANAGEMENT STYLE

When we were studying studying economics we were taught that the factors required for business could be expressed as 'four Ms': money, materials, machinery, men.

This seemed to imply that men are on a par with the other factors and just as incapable of independent thought and behaviour; and, indeed, the conventional wisdom of the time stated that 'managers think and workers work'. In a society where such concepts were taken for granted, autocratic management styles were regarded as appropriate. The all-knowing manager would make all decisions, define objectives and give the necessary instructions to his (never her) subordinate managers, who then ensured that the workforce carried out those instructions exactly. It was a case of pure 'management by fear'.

We have come a long way since those days. The most important change has been that the 'men' have declared that they are not on a par with the other factors and that they are capable of independent thought and action. Changes in the law, in social custom and in employee expectations have made 'management by fear' and other autocratic management styles increasingly ineffective.

Today's workforce responds to a different approach, one which could best be described as 'adult-to-adult' behaviour by the manager. This implies that the subordinate, who may not have the intelligence of his or her boss, nor the benefit of a higher education, is nevertheless an adult and is entitled to be treated as such. This concept underlies the participative management style, which is now regarded as the one most likely to evoke positive responses from subordinates.

Participative management

The participative style of management calls for the manager to see himself or herself not as someone who has a monopoly of knowledge and experience, but as a facilitator whose prime obligation is to help his or her subordinates do their jobs better. This does not imply 'soft management', whereby a pliant manager permits subordinates to avoid dealing with problems by 'delegating upwards', and fails to insist that they achieve objectives and agreed standards of quality. What it does imply has been described by a UK chief executive as 'tough love': a rigorous demand for results together with a caring and supportive attitude.

Participative management requires the manager to:

- Inform subordinates about company and departmental policies and objectives.
- Reach understanding with his or her subordinates about work-unit objectives and priorities.
- Involve subordinates in any process of planning, decision making or problem solving that relates to their daily work.
- Improve the process of communication within the work unit.
- Gain the commitment of his or her subordinates to achieving the objectives of their unit.

In daily behaviour the manager should give particular attention to:

- Emphasis on the achievement of objectives:
  — Defining and explaining the results which the unit must achieve.
  — Regularly comparing actual results with planned results.
  — Analysing, with his or her subordinates, the reasons for the difference between actual and planned results.
  — Praising and rewarding the achievement of results, not hard work.

- Team building (as described earlier).
- Facilitating the work of the unit.
- Supporting subordinates in the sense of preserving their self-esteem.

The last two points represent a major problem for many managers. We recall working with a pharmaceutical company in southern Europe, where the technical director was a formidable person, physically big, very authoritative and autocratic. He had two subordinates, one in charge of maintenance and the other in charge of production. During a workshop on objective-setting, the maintenance manager dared to ask for a copy of the annual production plan, so that he could prepare a plan for preventive maintenance. His boss brushed his request aside saying, 'You don't need a copy of the production plan.' The production manager then complained to the technical director that, despite the fact that a short time ago they had agreed on production objectives, he, the technical director, had since changed the objectives without any consultation, creating serious difficulties. The reply from the technical director was, 'Everybody has problems.'

Concerning subordinate support, it seems that many managers cannot resist the temptation of playing one-upmanship, deriding their subordinates' failures or (as we have seen) 'blowing their own trumpet' when they have been able to find a solution which eluded the subordinate. This kind of behaviour can only produce resentment and a desire for revenge. It is certainly counter-productive and unlikely to result in commitment to the unit or willingness to cooperate.

At its best, participative management results in a downward distribution of:

- *Power,* by giving subordinates a greater degree of autonomy.
- *Information* regarding the company as a whole and the particular department.
- *Knowledge and skills,* by giving subordinates the opportunity of personal growth through training and increased responsibilities.

Introducing the participative style of management to a company which practises a very different style is a very difficult and lengthy process, requiring much explanation and illustration, experiential learning and role-play. For many managers, it requires significant behavioural change. The pharmaceutical company which we mentioned earlier introduced a new era of participative management by putting an announcement on the notice-board, stating that from a certain date 'Participative management shall be practised in the company.' (We swear that this is true.) The managers of one department read the announcement, decided that it meant that there would be increases in salary, became very resentful when these did not appear and so decided to ignore the notice entirely!

We have found it useful to ask managers to remember the best and the worst boss they have ever had, and to describe each of them in three words. The characteristics of the best bosses are usually very similar, as are those of the worst bosses. We then ask them to participate in small-group discussions to develop a profile of 'the ideal manager'. Finally we ask them to use this profile as a kind of checklist to assess their own behaviour, and to develop action plans for personal improvement.

A frequent question is: Do attempts to introduce a similar pattern of behaviour for all managers produce 'photocopies' of some theoretically perfect manager and prevent natural behaviour? We believe that the answer is quite clear: there is no attempt to clone managers, but rather a perfectly legitimate demand from top management that all managers observe certain basic rules of behaviour, in order to develop and maintain a desired company culture. If managers are unable or unwilling to comply, they should seek their future elsewhere.

DEALING WITH CONFLICT

Conflict, both interdepartmental and interpersonal, seems to be an inevitable part of organizational life, but the energy thus wasted could have been spent on productive thought and activity. We have come across companies in which there is talk of 'constructive conflict': frankly, we see this as a contradiction in terms. We worked with a multinational company that manufactured in one country and marketed in others. The organizational structure was actually designed to generate 'creative conflict' between marketing and sales – they were independent departments accountable to different bosses. We cannot say that we observed any real benefit from this arrangement: enormous effort went on the never-ending disagreements between the two groups.

We are certainly not advocating a bland world in which there is never any disagreement and where everybody works in an atmosphere of suppressed emotions. We have seen the results of this, too. In the public works department of a German-speaking canton in Switzerland, when we asked why there was no system for performance evaluation of managers, the reply was 'nicht angenehm' ('not pleasant'). In an attempt to avoid any unpleasantness or conflict that might have resulted from critical comment, the department avoided using one of most important management tools, leaving people in a situation of polite uncertainty. In contrast, we remember a Danish company for whom we conducted a management audit by means of a comprehensive questionnaire, answered anonymously by all managers. Since Denmark has a very egalitarian society, and a tradition of non-autocratic management, the findings of the audit were positive. However, the section of the questionnaire dealing with conflict presented a very different picture: we found evidence of the most serious conflict between departments, management levels and individuals.

We believe that the correct approach to dealing with conflict involves two steps:

- Identifying the causes of potential conflict and doing everything possible to minimize outbreaks of unnecessary conflict.
- Dealing constructively with conflict when it does occur.

Before we look precisely at the causes of conflict, let us describe the groupings of forces in typical conflicts in manufacturing companies.

- *Production and Maintenance are always at loggerheads.* Production claim that 'they didn't fix it properly', or ask, 'How can we work when they always want the machinery down for preventive maintenance?' Maintenance claim that 'they didn't operate it properly', or ask, 'How can we do preventive maintenance when they refuse to stop the machines?'
- *Production and Maintenance join forces against Purchasing.* Production and Maintenance claim that 'Purchasing didn't order it properly', while Purchasing counter-claim that 'they didn't specify exactly what they wanted'.
- *Production, Maintenance and Purchasing complain about Marketing.* 'Marketing always want the biggest range of colours and sizes; they want a huge inventory, and they keep changing their minds.' Marketing complain bitterly that 'They are completely inflexible, and are unaware of and uninterested in changes in the market-place.'
- *The only thing on which Production, Maintenance, Purchasing and Marketing agree is how much they hate Finance.* 'They always say no.'

The causes of conflict

A few years ago, a study was made in America of potential sources of conflict in project-management situations. A large number of real cases were examined. The findings are set out here, with the sources of conflict in order of frequency.

- *Objectives*

This was the most frequent cause of conflict, which is to be expected because, inevitably, there will be serious differences of opinion as to what the company should be trying to achieve. There is, of course, the possibility that the differences stem from personal ambitions or animosities, or just from a manager's perception of his own importance. We observed this during a marketing planning session with a client company. A regional marketing manager was very resentful of the fact that his boss, the national marketing director, had the last word in determining the sales quota for his region. He claimed that since he knew the local conditions best, he should have the last word. When he was asked what happened when his own salesmen disagreed with him over sales quotas, claiming that they knew their local conditions best, his answer was that he could not work with such people.

- *Priorities*

Even if people agree about what the end-results should be, they may have very different opinions about what should be done first in order to achieve those objectives.

- *Responsibilities, authority, formal working relationships*

In our experience, this is a frequent cause of extreme interpersonal conflict, with claims and counter-claims: 'That's my job, not yours', or 'I make the decision on those matters, not you.' It results from lack of clarity in the definition of roles, as discussed in Chapter 4.

- *Technical options*

Objectives and priorities play a part here, and the conflict may well derive from sincere professional differences of opinion. Unfortunately, in some professions (of which medicine is one and architecture another) there is a curious lack of mutual professional respect, and each person disagrees with the others almost on principle. In situations where the collaboration of people from different scientific disciplines is required, disagreement is inevitable because of academic rivalry – after all, what theoretical physicist could agree with a mere life scientist? We have a friend who was appointed Professor of Environmental Protection at a Canadian university. He told us that his biggest problem had been to get the scientists from the various disciplines involved in environmental protection even to talk to one another.

- *Allocation of resources*

This appears as a source of conflict in the form of complaints: 'Why is his budget bigger than mine?' There are also very painful situations, for example, when research budgets have to be cut, either due to lack of funds or because a scientific breakthrough has not been achieved within the planned time and cost limits.

- *Costs*

Where actual costs have exceeded budgets recrimination often follows.

- *Schedules*

The allocation of time to different project activities can be a source of conflict between a project manager who wants things completed sooner, and members of the team who want more time.

- *Personalities*

In the US study, the clash of personalities ('I just don't like you') was the least frequent cause of conflict.

We found this study very interesting and feel that even though it was focused on project management it has validity in all organizations. In manufacturing industries, many conflicts could be avoided by team planning (described in Chapter 5) which provides opportunities for the airing of differences before work actually begins; and which carefully considers the implication of various options, thus minimizing differences of opinon that are based on purely emotional responses. A rigorous checking of the compatibility of departmental objectives and priorities should prevent clashes between department heads, each of whom believes that he or she is doing his or her best for the company, even though it is in direct contradiction to the efforts of others.

Unfortunately, conflict is often the result of circumstance which nobody tries to change. Two cases come to mind. In Greece, we had a client who manufactured carpets at a plant some 30 kilometres from Athens, while the administration and accounting was located in Athens itself. There was endless conflict between the plant and the office, whose only contact was by telephone. We believe that our most significant contribution was to insist on joint meetings between the two groups, who had never met each other personally. Each side suddenly discovered that the other was human after all, and that each had real problems. In Denmark, a high-technology company had separate marketing and sales departments, with a small advertising and public-relations unit attached to the marketing department. There were endless complaints by the sales people that advertising was out of touch with reality and always too late in preparing material. We believe that we solved the problem neatly by suggesting that the advertising and public-relations unit be transferred to the sales department, where it rapidly became an integral part of a much more effective operation.

Conflict and the behaviour of managers

It is useful to identify the different ways in which managers behave when trying to deal with unavoidable conflict.

- *Withdrawal*

This reaction ignores the conflict and hopes that it will go away. When working in a company with very serious interdepartmental conflict, we went to the president with an urgent plea to take some action, only to be told, 'Yes we know, we have been talking about it for a year.'

- *Smoothing*

This is the name given to attempts to minimize differences, but without really tackling major disagreements.

- *Compromising*

In wage negotiations, where the conflict results from disagreement between what the employer offers and the union wants, there is sometimes a solution in compromise. When there are differences about objectives, priorities, technical options, etc, compromise is not often possible or even desirable.

- *Forcing*

This describes the situation when one party, having greater power than the other, enforces its opinion without any real consideration of what is needed. Forcing is a very unsatisfactory way of resolving conflict because it results in what is called a 'win/lose' situation, leaving the 'Winner' with the satisfaction of triumph and the 'Loser' with the humiliation of defeat. This is all very well in a real competitive situation, where the parties may never see each other again, but is inappropriate and most undesirable when the parties must continue to work together. The loser retreats, wounded in dignity and full of resentment and planning revenge, or refusing to implement the decision.

- *Confrontation*

This seems to be the only constructive way of dealing with conflict. It means recognizing that there are real differences, and insisting on analysing them in as realistic, considered and unemotional manner as possible, thus preserving the self-esteem of both parties and achieving a solution which could be described as 'win/win'. Even if one side has been obliged to concede, its dignity remains intact.

MAKING EVERYONE A WINNER

This is a very evocative phrase but we do seriously believe that it expresses the essence of good management. We accept as valid the concept that a person performs and achieves (or fails to achieve) in accordance with his or her self-image. There is no doubt that 'losers lose': people with a very poor image of themselves, who believe that they will 'lose', will, by some instinct, say or do the wrong thing and prevent themselves from succeeding, even though they are trying very hard to succeed. It is equally true that 'winners win': one of the most important aspects of sports training is to help athletes to 'psyche themselves up' before the race.

The story of the turn-around of National Carriers in the UK is a proof of this concept. National Carriers was a government-owned transport company, employing some 12 000 people and operating a fleet of about 8000 lorries. It was operating in the most hostile of business environments – a depressed economy, very serious competition, heavy trade-union intervention – and it was losing £10 million every year. The new managing director was able to change the regular loss into an annual profit of four million pounds. The business environment remained as hostile as ever; no new people were brought in (in fact, one complete layer of managers was fired); and there was no help from the government. We believe that the secret of this amazing achievement was the management's ability to get the employees, who had seen themselves as losers, to see themselves as winners. The managing director and his team changed the organization's structure, making it less top-heavy and bureaucratic. They gave much more autonomy to branch managers, making them responsible for setting and achieving their own objectives; and they created an entrepreneurial climate throughout the whole company.

When working with the US Army in Europe (USAREUR) we observed the same thing. In a totally bureaucratic organization which was subject to the most rigid regulations and where the manager of an administrative unit had no possibility of giving any kind of material reward for achievement, there were some units whose performance was significantly greater than others. The explanation could only lie in the management style in those units. We were enormously impressed with one manager who said, 'My biggest problem was convincing my people how good they are'; and with another who said, 'My unit had so many problems that I did not know what to do – until *we* brainstormed all night and found a way.'

There is a concept known as the 'Pygmalion effect'. In Greek mythology, Pygmalion was a king of Cyprus who fell in love with a statue of Aphrodite. Ovid modified the story, and wrote about Pygmalion, a sculptor, who fell in love with a statue of his own creation. Bernard Shaw used the idea when he wrote *Pygmalion,* a play in which Professor Higgins creates a lady of Eliza Doolittle, a poor flower-girl, by teaching her how to speak proper English and convincing her that she is a 'lady'. Now the 'Pygmalion effect' is the name for the effect that a teacher, parent or manager can have on the achievements of a child or subordinate, by expressing high expectations and then convincing the subordinate that he or she is capable of reaching them. A number of cases illustrate this concept.

Some psychologists once arrived unexpectedly at a school in America and announced that they had come to carry out intelligence tests on the children. They carried out the tests, did not show the results to the teachers, but told them that certain children (whom they named) had great potential and were 'late bloomers'. About a year later the same psychologists reappeared to repeat the tests. The children who had been identified as 'late bloomers' achieved significant improvements over their own previous results. These children had, in fact, been selected completely at random and had shown no particular promise. It was only because their teachers believed that they did have potential, and began to treat them accordingly, that they were able to improve so dramatically.

The second case comes from the Second World War, when America was trying to speed up its shipbuilding programme in response to the German U-boats' successful torpedoing of allied shipping. The shipbuilding programme depended on the availability of a large number of skilled welders, so a crash training programme had to be conducted. At the beginning of the course the instructor selected a number of people who did seem to show some natural ability, and continually referred to them as examples for the other students. By the time the course was half over, the selected students had already achieved the necessary level of skill. Once again, it was the expectations of the instructor together with the continual reinforcement of his behaviour towards them that enabled those students to achieve what they did.

One other aspect of self-perception is relevant here: 'taking responsibility for oneself'. Many people see themselves as victims of circumstances beyond their control – 'leaves blown in the wind'. This is a very convenient attitude: good things can be attributed to luck or effort, but when things go wrong it is always somebody else's fault. For a company, the implications of this kind of attitude are very serious. Individual employees or managers will always find excuses for poor results and, as this behaviour spreads – and it will – the company as a whole may begin to see itself as subject to the whims of fortune. What is required is the very opposite of this: an attitude of taking responsibility and believing that one is not the victim of circumstances but capable of influencing the events in one's life. It was Sir Alistair Pilkington, the chairman of Pilkington Glass, who said in his retirement speech: 'For a company to survive, it must cope with the future. For a company to prosper, it must create the future.'

All this suggests that managers can have a significant influence over the self-perception of their subordinates and, as a consequence, over their ability to achieve.

Chapter 7

Management Awareness

The productive organization is one which is continually active in self-monitoring and self-correction, and which operates in a climate of never-ending self-improvement. There are two requirements for effective self-correction and self-improvement:

- Awareness of what is going on both outside and inside the company.
- Ability to respond promptly and effectively to changing circumstances. It is often necessary to initiate changes in the company in advance of anticipated external changes.

EXTERNAL DATA

In a world of constant change and increasing competition, it is essential to develop a company-wide ability to think strategically. This means that the focus of everybody's thinking should be primarily outside the company, on economic trends, on markets, customers and competitors, on the possible implications for the company, and on developing a sustainable competitive advantage. For sales and marketing people, looking outside may be second nature. People in the production, accounting and personnel departments usually have to focus on internal factors and have no opportunity to participate in discussions on the wider business environment. Given the chance, these people are delighted to be involved and have many ideas to contribute. We cannot recommend too strongly that every effort be made, both in team-planning sessions and in periodic briefings, to involve people from all departments in discussions relating to external factors.

Economics

Obviously, economic factors must be watched: price levels, interest rates, credit policy, etc. All have direct impact on customers' desire and ability to buy, and on the company's ability to perform. It is important to identify those key indicators which are most relevant to the company's activities, and to monitor them closely. We remember a plate-glass manufacturer who followed the statistics on building completions (not building starts, which we would have expected) because he believed that this was a more accurate and sensitive indicator of future demand for window glass.

Social factors

Social factors relate to the size and structure of the population, its working and living habits, and its values and priorities. The trend in the UK of increasing home ownership, the 'gentrification' of old blocks of flats, and the home-improvement and do-it-yourself boom, are typical examples of social trends which are significant for many industries.

Politics

Changing political trends; the implementation of government programmes (in the UK, the privatization of nationalized industries and government support for an enterprise economy; in France, the nationalization of large companies); and even the anticipation of future government policy, are all factors which must be taken into account as part of a 'macro' view of the company's business environment.

Technological change

This was discussed in the section, *Improving planning* (see page 40–42).

Legislation

Changes in the law can have a significant impact on a company's operations. Product liability and environmental protection regulations are currently of particular concern. We know of a firm of lawyers in Brussels whose main activity is advising multinational clients of anticipated European Community legislation, so that they can take appropriate action.

Internationalization

The growing internationalization of business creates new opportunities and new threats, some of which are not immediately obvious. The 1992 Single Market programme of the European Community is a case in point, particularly since it includes a new form of collaboration between the EC and the European Free Trade Association (EFTA) to create a 'European space'. We are currently working on strategic planning with a large food manufacturer in Finland, and as part of the planning process have been looking at possible changes in the business environment. Since Finland is a member of EFTA, the president of the company arranged for a short lecture on the implications of the programme to be given to the planning group by an economist from the Finnish Food Manufacturers Association. The lecture revealed aspects of the new situation of which the group had been completely unaware.

Markets

When we conduct planning workshops with clients we always ask, 'Do you feel you know enough about your markets, customers and competitors?' Inevitably, the answer is a sorrowful, 'No, not nearly enough.' Yet, when we pursue the question and ask whether they think they could find out a great deal more if they were to apply themselves, the answer is usually in the affirmative. We sincerely believe that it is possible to obtain significant information without major investment in market research. (This is not meant to imply that we are against market research, we merely state that companies can do a great deal with their own resources.)

In order to plan, it is necessary to understand the structure of the market and the factors which influence it. The information required includes the following:

- Market size, in terms of buying potential.
- The major companies in the market.
- Market shares of the major companies.
- The financial state of the major companies.
- The number of competitors in the industry (is the industry fragmented or concentrated?).
- The number of potential buyers in the market.
- An assessment of the bargaining power of suppliers.
- An assessment of the bargaining power of buyers.
- An assessment of the threat of potential new entrants to the industry.
- An assessment of the threat of possible substitute products or services.
- Overall trends in local sales, imports and exports.
- Recent developments (new products, technical advances, company takeovers and liquidations).
- An assessment of the future prospects of the industry.

We have a friend in the UK who left a senior position with a large manufacturing company to go into business for himself. He carried out surveys of a number of different industries, using the kind of analysis suggested above, and identified one which is highly fragmented, offers products and services to a very large number of diversified buyers, and has a reputation for non-professional management, under-utilization of plant capacity and low profitability. He decided that in such an industry there were opportunities for buying a company cheaply, and for making significant profits. Furthermore, since the industry is so fragmented, his greater profitability would not provoke retaliatory action by competitors. He was able to buy a company, and is proving just how right he was in his analysis.

Customers

Companies claim to be 'customer oriented', but in fact it is often lip-service that is paid to this fine-sounding idea. Just how far most companies are from being really customer oriented is indicated by the articles that have started to appear in business journals, with titles such as 'Rediscovering the customer', 'Closer to the customer', and even 'Love the customer'. Customer orientation means trying to understand the customer's needs and motivations, and to see the company's products and services through the customer's eyes. To show how refined this kind of research into customer motivation can become, we can quote a Finnish market research company which has identified about 20 different motivations for eating bread! Customer orientation also means going to almost any lengths to satisfy the customer and give him or her the feeling of getting value for money. It means 'delivering as promised' (something that house builders and home-improvement contractors seem unable to do); and finding out why loyal customers are loyal, why they come back a second time. And, equally important, what accounts for the loyalty of people who remain the customers of the competition?

Competitors

Analysing the competition is an essential part of strategic and market planning. To develop realistic and appropriate marketing plans it is necessary to define market needs, estimate the company's share of the market, assess the relative strengths and weaknesses of both the company and the competition, and try to anticipate competitors' reactions to the company's own proposed strategies. Much has already been written about this – we have even heard of an American company that appointed a 'vice-president of competitive analysis'.

Despite the interest, not nearly enough is done, systematically, to obtain and update information on competitors. A company in the English Midlands, engaged in marketing industrial products, took our advice and obtained the published accounts of some of its competitors. The competitors proved to be far more profitable. Although very much jolted by this discovery, the company was able to implement a series of actions to improve margins and reduce costs.

Without resorting to spying, a great deal of information can be obtained fairly easily from two main sources.

- *Field data*

Much of this can be obtained by the company's employees during the course of their daily activities, especially from the sales force, who are out on the road, visit distributors' premises and talk to their employees. Sales people see competitors' products, packaging and promotional material; can obtain information on competitors' pricing policy and terms of payment; and see the amount of shelf-space given by distributors to their own as compared with rival products. Trade gossip is inevitable and so some information can be obtained just by asking leading questions. The important point is that this data collection should not be done at random; it must be a defined and integral part of every salesman's job. A written report on every sales visit must be submitted, answering specific questions in a given format so that the data can be entered into a data bank and analysed at regular intervals. Some salesmen resist collecting data and writing reports, claiming that their only job is to sell. This resistance must be overcome.

We remember a cosmetics manufacturer in Greece, in whose head office there was one office with its door always locked, provoking our curiosity. One day, walking down the corridor, we spotted that the door was open, and could not resist the temptation of looking inside. All that was to be seen was a little old man, writing in a huge old-fashioned ledger. He was keeping a hand-written record of the prices of all competing products in every perfumery in Athens. The astounding thing was that his records were completely up-to-date on a daily basis. We never found out how he got his information, and decided that the Oracle at Delphi was probably still providing answers!

Other internal sources of market and competitor information are maintenance and repairmen, who provide after-sales service and thus come into regular contact with technical people from customer companies. The purchasing department may be in a position to get information from suppliers regarding the types and quantities of materials bought by competitors, and very important, how consistent those competitors are in paying their bills.

Many external sources of competitor information are available. Market-research firms and advertising agencies can be assigned to obtain information; and security analysts, trade associations and friendly bankers can also be valuable. Attendance at professional and trade meetings provides opportunities for collecting titbits about competitors.

To summarize, there is a great deal of information about competitors and the market dispersed between many people in the company. The trick is to collect it systematically into one 'bank', and have it regularly updated and analysed for planning purposes.

- *Published data*

Every limited liability company is obliged to file an abridged version of its annual accounts at Companies House, giving the minimum information required by the Companies Act. These annual accounts are available for public scrutiny against payment of a small fee. The published data may not be as comprehensive as analysts would like; nevertheless they do give important clues about the performance and financial condition of competing firms.

Speeches by chief executives are published in the press, also articles about their companies. Local newspapers often report on company happenings. Employment advertisements (where the name of the company is disclosed) can give clues. Patent registrations and court records are also open to inspection.

Owner relations

For managers of publicly owned companies, an awareness of owner attitudes is essential, particularly when takeovers are so prevalent. *Fortune* magazine reports that in America, litigation has led to shareholders reasserting their rights to control the companies which they own, rather than leaving ultimate decision-making power in the hands of the chief executive. This is very uncomfortable for erstwhile all-powerful chief executives, and for boards of directors who tended to give rubber-stamp approval.

Government relations

While not on the same level of importance as customer and competitor information, we feel that companies should be aware of how they are perceived by local government and by those government departments with which they come in contact. Is the company perceived as a good employer, a non-polluter, an asset to the local area? Is it regarded as professionally and financially honest?

INTERNAL DATA

Operating results

In Chapter 5, under the heading *Improving control* (pages 42–46) we discussed reporting requirements. Since this chapter focuses on management awareness, we would like to emphasize two points:

- The need for up-to-date financial and non-financial data, presented in a form and in terms which are meaningful to operating managers.
- The need to involve as many managers as possible, from all departments, in the analysis and interpretation of results.

We can quote two relevant cases. The first is that of a large government-owned housing company, whose task was the collection of rents and maintenance of properties. The monthly financial report to managers (on a departmental basis) showed the amount budgeted for each expense item, the departmental budgeted total, and actual expenses expressed as a percentage of the budget. There was no indication whatever of planned and actual results in real terms. This meant that a manager could learn, for example, that in half a year he had spent 60 per cent of his budget and had only 40 per cent left. What he had actually achieved with the money spent, and what remained to be done, was not mentioned. The second case is of an arms manufacturer, where a young member of the accounting department asked to be allowed to sit in at monthly meetings to review financial results. He was told that he was not 'senior enough' to participate.

Employee attitudes

Information about employee attitudes should be very important to management. Unfortunately, traditional reporting collects only hard facts, and data which deal with feelings and perceptions are often ignored. Also, it is difficult to collect such data and express the findings in a quantified way which facilitates comparisons over a period of time. We use a comprehensive questionnaire as a survey instrument. The questions are presented as positive statements describing an ideal situation. The respondents express their opinions by marking an option code-number. The options are: strongly agree; inclined to agree; no opinion; inclined to disagree; strongly disagree. The questionnaire is completed anonymously by all employees, but they give the code-number of their department or unit. A computer program counts the replies to each option for each question, and prints a separate 'profile' of employees' attitudes in each unit. Figure 7.1 shows an example of a typical computer print-out. The column headed 'opinions' gives raw data: the numbers of replies to each question. The column headed 'percentages' gives the different opinions as percentages of the total. The column headed 'index' gives the weighted average of the replies to each question. This document provides a quantified summary of the feelings and perceptions of the employees as expressed by them and not by an outsider. We will elaborate on this in Chapter 8.

```
┌──────────────────────────────────────────────────────────────────────────────────┐
│                                                                                    │
│ JACOBS-MANAGEMENT CONSULTANTS    TOTALS REPORT FOR—MANAGEMENT AUDIT  PAGE—71        │
│ *****************************    ********************************    DATE—8/04/86   │
│                                                                                    │
│      COMPANY PROFILE                  COMPANY—                                      │
│                                       ********                                      │
│                                                                                    │
│        O  P  I  N  I  O  N  S      PERCENTAGES         I  N  D  E  X                │
│        --------------------------  --------------      ----------------             │
│                                                                                    │
│  QUESTION  5   4   3   2   1   0   T   5+4    3    2+1    0   5.4.3.2.1.0   AVERAGE  │
│  ********  *** *** *** *** *** *** *** ***   ***   ***   ***  -----------  *******  │
│  1.01.01   22  16   4   2          44  86.4   9.1   4.5        *              4.3    │
│  1.01.02   18  18   1   7          44  81.8   2.3  15.9        *              4.1    │
│  1.01.03    6  25   5   8          44  70.5  11.4  18.2         *             3.7    │
│  1.01.04    9  22   5   5   2   1  44  70.5  11.4  15.9   2.3   *             3.6    │
│  1.01.05   10  23   9   2          44  75.0  20.5   4.5        *              3.9    │
│  1.01.06   13  22   3   5   1      44  79.5   6.8  13.6        *              3.9    │
│  1.01.07   14  19   6   5          44  75.0  13.6  11.4        *              4.0    │
│  1.01.08   13  18  11   2          44  70.5  25.0   4.5        *              4.0    │
│  1.01.09   15  16   6   7          44  70.5  13.6  15.9        *              3.9    │
│  1.01.10   14  15   4  11          44  65.9   9.1  25.0         *             3.7    │
│  1.01.11   12  14  13   5          44  59.1  29.5  11.4         *             3.8    │
│  1.01.12   10  12   7  12   3      44  50.0  15.9  34.1         *             3.3    │
│  1.01.13    6  19  10   6   3      44  56.8  22.7  20.5         *             3.4    │
│  1.02.01    8  25   5   6          44  75.0  11.4  13.6         *             3.8    │
│  1.02.02   14   9  13   6   2      44  52.3  29.5  18.2         *             3.6    │
│  1.02.03   12  14  11   6   1      44  59.1  25.0  15.9         *             3.7    │
│  1.02.04    5  10  20   5   4      44  34.1  45.5  20.5          *            3.2    │
│  1.02.05   12  13  15   3   1      44  56.8  34.1   9.1         *             3.7    │
│  1.02.06   14  11  14   4   1      44  56.8  31.8  11.4        *              3.8    │
│  1.02.07    8   8  10  11   7      44  36.4  22.7  40.9          *            3.0    │
│  1.02.08   11  12  13   6   2      44  52.3  29.5  18.2         *             3.5    │
│  1.02.09   17  14   7   5   1      44  70.5  15.9  13.6        *              3.9    │
│  1.02.10    7  18  11   7       1  44  56.8  25.0  15.9   2.3   *             3.5    │
│  1.02.11    5  12  21   4       2  44  38.6  47.7   9.1   4.5   *             3.3    │
│  1.02.12    5  11  22   5       1  44  36.4  50.0  11.4   2.3   *             3.3    │
│                                                                                    │
└──────────────────────────────────────────────────────────────────────────────────┘
```

Figure 7.1 *Typical computer print-out*

111

Chapter 8

Diagnosing Symptoms

The main theme of this chapter is 'ownership': the feeling among the managers and employees of a company that any company problems are 'their' problems, that the analysis of those problems is 'their' analysis, and that plans for the solution of the problems are 'their' plans. This sense of ownership is essential for real commitment to implementing necessary change. Without it, the identification of problems and any attempts to analyse causes and find solutions are likely to produce resentment, and defence against what is perceived as criticism. Real commitment can only be attained by involving managers and employees actively in the process, and by sharing with them the feeling of success in solving the problems.

We give here one case which illustrates the difficulties in obtaining collaboration, and a second which illustrates how managers can create situations which militate against future cooperation. The first case is of a UK knitwear factory which faced demands for wage increases at a time when it was in serious financial difficulties. The managing director told us that he had shown the workers the latest financial statements, and had explained that paying increased wages could actually bankrupt the company. The reply was, 'That's your problem.' The second case is that of General Motors in America, which suspended profit-sharing payments to union workers, as part of a cost-cutting campaign, and immediately afterwards awarded salary increases to executives.

On the other hand, we know a Finnish family-owned company which sends a copy of the annual financial accounts to the home of every employee, and in which the chief executive meets with the trade union representatives to present results and answer questions prior to the public release of the information. The employees and their representatives respond very favourably to this behaviour.

The secondary theme of this chapter is the need for rigorous examination of financial and non-financial data on a regular and frequent basis. This sounds obvious, but we often come across companies that try to operate without monthly management accounts or any kind of useful regular analysis. In discussions with managers about weaknesses in their systems lack of information and inadequate control mechanisms are frequently mentioned.

ANALYSING FINANCIAL RESULTS

Much has been written about the analysis of financial statements and we do not presume to add to existing knowledge. What seems to us to be important is not so much the techniques of analysis, but understanding the implications and responding promptly. The UK investment company, 3i (Investors in Industry) has been quoted in the *Journal of the Institute of Directors* as saying that many companies pass the point of rescue because they seek help too late. We are not discussing companies in distress but the point of early response is still valid.

These are the early-warning signals which are potentially significant:

- Volume of sales reduced when compared with planned volume, or with sales during a similar period in past years, or with the sales of competitors.

- Slow growth in sales compared with projections, or in relation to key market indicators, or in relation to overall sales in the industry, as reported by trade associations.

- The appearance of cash-flow problems that make it difficult to meet obligations as they fall due.

- Reduced monthly profits, or even the first appearance of monthly losses.

While recommending prompt reaction, we do recognize the danger of over-reacting and creating unnecessary panic. Quoting again from the article by 3i, 'How do you distinguish the temporary hiccup from the terminal decline?' Our advice is: make people aware of the facts and the possible implications, monitor results more frequently, and start an investigation of possible causes by teams drawn from all the departments that have any connection with the problem.

At the risk of repeating the obvious, we suggest monthly financial reporting to facilitate an integrated form of analysis, which should be discussed with all operating managers. This analysis should include the following elements, and should present current and comparative figures. (In the given example, in the interests of simplicity and clarity, we have used abbreviated numbers and have not shown comparative figures.)

Earning power

Operating income:
$$\frac{\text{EBIT (Earnings before interest and tax)}}{\text{Total assets}} \quad \frac{4000}{31\,000} = 12.90\%$$

Earnings before tax:	$\dfrac{\text{EBT}}{\text{Total assets}}$	$\dfrac{3000}{31\,000}$	= 9.70%
Return on investment:	$\dfrac{\text{Net income}}{\text{Total assets}}$	$\dfrac{1800}{31\,000}$	= 5.80%
Return on equity:	$\dfrac{\text{Net income}}{\text{Equity}}$	$\dfrac{1800}{10\,300}$	= 17.50%

Profitability

$\dfrac{\text{Cost of sales}}{\text{Sales}}$	$\dfrac{38\,000}{51\,000}$	= 74.50%
$\dfrac{\text{Gross profit}}{\text{Sales}}$	$\dfrac{13\,000}{51\,000}$	= 25.50%
$\dfrac{\text{Operating expenses}}{\text{Sales}}$	$\dfrac{9000}{51\,000}$	= 17.65%
$\dfrac{\text{EBIT}}{\text{Sales}}$	$\dfrac{4000}{51\,000}$	= 7.85%
$\dfrac{\text{Interest}}{\text{Sales}}$	$\dfrac{1000}{51\,000}$	= 1.96%
$\dfrac{\text{Net income}}{\text{Sales}}$	$\dfrac{8000}{51\,000}$	= 15.69%

Asset management

Total asset turnover:	$\dfrac{\text{Sales}}{\text{Total assets}}$	$\dfrac{51\,000}{31\,000}$	$\dfrac{1.645}{1}$
Fixed asset turnover:	$\dfrac{\text{Sales}}{\text{Fixed assets}}$	$\dfrac{51\,000}{7000}$	$\dfrac{7.286}{1}$
Inventory turnover:	$\dfrac{\text{Cost of sales}}{\text{Inventory}}$	$\dfrac{38\,000}{12\,000}$	$\dfrac{3.167}{1}$
Debtors turnover:	$\dfrac{\text{Credit sales}}{\text{Debtors}}$	$\dfrac{51\,000}{10\,000}$	$\dfrac{5.10}{1}$

Financing

Sources of finance

	£	% of total assets
Current liabilities	10 000	32.30%
Long-term liabilities	10 700	34.50%
Total liabilities	20 700	66.80%
Shareholders' equity	10 300	33.20%
Total assets	31 000	100.00%

Financing charges

$$\frac{\text{Interest}}{\text{Total liabilities}} \qquad \frac{1000}{20\ 700} = 4.83\%$$

$$\frac{\text{Interest}}{\text{Short-term liabilities}} \qquad \frac{600}{10\ 000} = 6.00\%$$

$$\frac{\text{Interest}}{\text{Long-term liabilities}} \qquad \frac{400}{10\ 700} = 3.74\%$$

Liquidity

Current ratio: $\dfrac{\text{Current assets}}{\text{Current liabilities}} \qquad \dfrac{24\ 000}{10\ 000} = \dfrac{2.40}{1}$

Acid test: $\dfrac{\text{Current assets less inventories}}{\text{Current liabilities}} \qquad \dfrac{12\ 000}{10\ 000} = \dfrac{1.20}{1}$

Continuous improvement in overall profitability will only be achieved by attacking each of these elements separately:

- *Gross profit margins* Marketing and sales must achieve the best possible selling prices, and the most profitable product mix.
- *Operating profits:* Manufacturing must seek the most cost-effective production methods.
- *Asset management:* Everybody must be involved in finding ways to operate with the lowest investment in current and fixed assets.

The following example, which uses the so-called Du Pont formula and the numbers used earlier, illustrates the point.

	EBIT	×	Sales	=	EBIT
	Sales		Total assets		Total assets

Existing situation	$\dfrac{4000}{51\ 000}$	×	$\dfrac{51\ 000}{31\ 000}$	=	$\dfrac{4000}{31\ 000}$
	7.84%	×	1.645/1	=	12.90%

Improve profitability on sales	$\dfrac{5000}{51\ 000}$	×	$\dfrac{51\ 000}{31\ 000}$	=	$\dfrac{5000}{31\ 000}$
	9.80%	×	1.645/1	=	16.12%

The profitability on sales has been improved (from 4000 to 5000) by reducing the costs of production. The sales volume remains the same, as does the asset management ratio (Sales/Total Assets). The operating income ratio (EBIT/Total Assets) has been improved from 12.9 to 16.12 per cent.

Improve Asset management	$\dfrac{4000}{51\ 000}$	×	$\dfrac{51\ 000}{20\ 000}$	=	$\dfrac{4000}{20\ 000}$
	7.84%	×	2.55/1	=	20.00%

The asset management ratio has been improved, by reducing the investment in assets from 31 000 to 20 000 (say, by reducing the level of inventories), while maintaining the same level of sales and of profitability on sales. The operating income ratio has been improved from 12.9 to 20.0 per cent.

The examples illustrate that the two components of the Du Pont formula can be dealt with independently, and that improving asset management can have a more significant effect on the final Operating Income Ratio (and ultimately on Return on Investment), than improving the percentage of profit on sales. The ideal is, of course, to improve both components.

PERIODICAL REPORTS

As discussed in Chapter 5, the essence of any control system is comparing actual results with desired results and, if necessary, carrying out immediate corrective actions. This requires definition of appropriate criteria for measurement, to take account of the following:

- Factors directly related to achieving the objectives (primary operational activities). These include all the variables which are controllable by managers. They should be expressed in terms of:
  — Revenues and costs (financial data).
  — Outputs and inputs (non-financial data). Essentially, these relate to logistics, operations, quality, marketing, sales and promotion service.
- Factors which are not directly related to operations and sales, but which are important parts of the 'value chain'. These are the various support activities, including corporate headquarters, financial management, human-resource management, procurement, technology development.

The overall constraint on any control system is the 'cost of costing'. This means that the system itself must be cost-effective, economically generating significant data. Under-control will result in lack of information; over-control will generate too much information.

Let us look in more detail at the criteria for measurement for each factor.

Sales

Sales data are often reported globally (that is, total sales for each period). Such data are interesting in a general way but they are not useful for control purposes. For sales data to be really useful, they should be broken down by:

- salesmen;
- geographical location;
- market segment;
- product line;
- credit sales/cash sales.

We have noted an accounting routine practice which may be convenient but which is very misleading. When discounts are given, the amount is deducted from the value of the invoice and the net amount is credited to the sales account. We believe that this understates and distorts sales figures and hides the significance of the discounts. To obtain accurate sales figures and a basis for judging discount policy, sales should aways be recorded 'gross' and a separate record kept for discounts.

We have worked with a Greek biscuit manufacturer whose salesmen were held responsible for both sales and collections. The accounting system recorded collections by each salesman separately, since commission was paid on cash collected and not on sales invoices. In this case, the accounting data served both as a very effective control mechanism and also as an incentive to the salesmen.

Marketing, advertising and promotion, selling

Whereas production costs are usually very carefully controlled, the opposite is often true of the costs of marketing, advertising and promotion, and selling. Since these activities take place outside the company's premises they are regarded as less measurable and therefore less controllable.

Marketing costs relate to market research, analysis of the competition, segmentation studies, etc, and should be planned and budgeted for no less rigorously than production costs. The difficulty lies in defining desired results in a measurable way, and the relevant costs of different levels of activity.

We have worked with a company in New York which has no production activities at all, being involved in worldwide merchandising of fashion goods. They have developed their own version of management by objectives – they call it 'BBO' (budgeting by objectives) – whereby each manager is required to prepare a form entitled 'Management by objectives – Description of objective' (Figure 8.1) for each main objective of his or her unit (expense centre). The form describes:

- the objective;
- the plan for implementing the objective;
- the results of implementing the objective;
- means of measuring implementation;
- the total cost.

The manager of the expense centre is then required to summarize all the 'Description of objective' forms on to a 'Budget worksheet' (Figure 8.2), on which the total cost is broken down by expense-account number. Since each expense centre has its own expense account, an accurate record can be kept of actual expenses in relation to budget, and in relation to actual results.

Advertising and promotion expenses are even more difficult to control. There is an old saying, 'Half our advertising budget is wasted, but we don't know which half.' Part of the problem lies in the difficulty of budgeting in relation to desired results – the other part lies in measuring the actual impact of the advertising.

In an attempt to improve advertising planning and budgeting, the British Business Press, an association representing various publishers, has offered recommendations regarding business-to-business advertising. We include copies of several of their checklists (Figures 8.3–8.7).

However, this still leaves many difficult questions unanswered. For example, 'What is the return on my advertising investment?', What is the optimum budget?', 'How much advertising is enough?' The larger advertising agencies have developed a measuring tool called 'econometrics', a form of statistical analysis which measures sales patterns against advertising and other marketing forces. By monitoring past performance, it is claimed that it can:

Fiscal Year:	Exp. Center Number:	Expense Center Name:		Approved by:	Initials:
				Chairman	
Prepared by (Name & Position):			Date:	Group Officer	
				Divisional	

Obj. No.	Objective:

Plan for Implementing Objective (Include Names &/or Titles of Current & New Personnel):

Results of Implementing Objective (Benefits, Consequences, Necessary Reorganizations):

Means of Measuring Implementation of Objective:

	Progress Reviews (Dates):		Total Cost
* Enter after completing	Scheduled	Actual	
MBO – Budget Worksheet.			

Figure 8.1 *Management by objectives: description of objective*

119

Fiscal Year:	Expense Center Number:	Expense Center Name:	Prepared by (Name & Position):

Obj. No.	Title of Objective (from MBO – Description of Objective form)	000	011		021	031	037	041	045	061	062	070
		#										
		#										
		#										
		#										
		#										
		#										
		#										
		#										
		#										
		#										
		#										
		#										
		#										
Totals by Classification		#										

Figure 8.2 *Management by objectives: budget worksheet*

| Medium | Last year | | Current year | | Person/dept |
	Budget	Actual	Budget	Actual	responsible
Business Press					
National Press					
Local Press					
Brochures					
Catalogues etc					
Exhibitions					
Direct Mail					
Public Relations					
Directories					
Video/AV					
Sponsorship					
Premiums					
Production					
Fees					
Other					

Figure 8.3 *Publicity budget real cost analysis*

Competitor Company

Product/Service

	Estimated expenditure*	Main titles/sites used
Business Press	£	
National Press	£	
Exhibitions	£	
Other Media	£	

* Often very difficult but your competitor will be using similar media and your sales force and the media will know.

CONTENT ANALYSIS
(for main medium only)

Main product claim

Proof/evidence for claims

Stated customer benefits

Visual theme

Requested customer action

N.B. Complete a form for each major competitor and company's own product/service.

Completed by   Date

Figure 8.4   *Competitive advertising analysis for year: estimated budgets*

1. What is the overall marketing strategy?

- Increase sales of current product/service by £X000s – by expanding the market.
- Increase market share by taking sales from competitors.
- Launch new product.
- Widen customer base.
- Create qualified sales leads.
- Change attitude to company.
- Increase awareness of company.

2. What am I advertising?

- An existing product/service.
- A product range.
- A new product.
- A new aspect of the company/product.
- A competitive, relevant image for the company.
- An offer of information or demonstration etc.

3. To whom am I advertising?

- Which types of business employ them?
- What size of company?
- What title?
- What job function?
- Where are they located?
- How many are there?
- How often must I reach them to be effective? Quote sources for these judgements – market research sales records, analysis of response, exhibition records etc.

4. What do I want to achieve?

- New product launch.
- Provide detailed information.
- Reach specific target audience.
- Create effective sales leads.
- Increase product awareness among target.
- Have the right business environment.
- Provide effective sales support.
- Increase company reputation.
- Broaden customer base.
- Provide cost effective advertising.
- Communicate detailed information.
- Product demonstration.

5. What customer benefit do I offer?

- Is it competitive?
- Is it relevant?

- Will it change attitudes or awareness positively?
- Will it be news?
- Can I prove it?
- Can I deliver it?
- Can it be used to enhance the company, as well as product sales?

Justify against competitive analysis, customer feedback. Ensure that the product benefit is valuable and relevant to customers and expressed in their language.

6. What action do I want?

- Phone call/letter.
- Request for more information.
- Identified visit to my exhibition stand.
- New awareness of my product/service.
- Positive change of opinion.
- Increase in my company's reputation etc.
- Internal discussion in prospect company.
- Review of existing buying practice.
- Opportunity to quote.
- Clipping and filing for future reference.
- New sale and repeat order.

7. How can I check if the advertising works?

i. Response
- Have I planned to record the following information?
    date received
    source of enquiry*
    action taken
    customer reaction
    follow up
    sales result
*e.g. For a press advertisement record magazine title, date, specific advertisement, colour, b/w, page cost etc. for future planning purposes.
ii. Communication
- Have I pre-tested the advertising concepts for communication of the key points in the advertising brief?
iii. Opinions
- Have I researched current attitudes and opinions of the company product/service and is a check on changes planned for next year?
This data will be used to plan future promotion.

Figure 8.5 *Advertising objectives: key headings and some options*

123

1. Check types for overall relevance

i.   Business to business – professional technical news magazines, product magazines, trade and retail publications, international magazines.
ii. National and regional newspapers, and freesheets.
iii. Directories and year books.
iv. Other.

WHICH TYPES WILL BEST MEET MY PRIMARY ADVERTISING OBJECTIVES?

- New product launch.
- Provide detailed information.
- Reach specific target groups.
- Create effective sales leads.
- Increase product awareness among target.
- Have the right business environment.
- Provide effective sales support.
- Increase company reputation.
- Broaden customer base.
- Provide cost effective advertising.
- Communicate detailed information.
- Product demonstration.

2. Check media benefits against objectives

For the medium:

i.   Deliver specific selected target groups and allow precise economic targeting.
ii. Cover the selected market in depth reaching all people involved in decision making.
iii. Deliver the advertisement in a relevant business environment.
iv. Allow an effective level of frequency.

3. Check specific magazine title against cost targets, advertising objectives and total promotion integration.

- Does the circulation and readership match my target audience definition in detail?
- Is the editorial content of proven interest to potential customers?
- In what depth does the magazine cover my business interest?
- What level of pass-on readership is there?
- What reader response services are available?
- What opportunities are there for integration with the rest of my promotion programme?
- What other services are offered that will be useful to me?
- Check publisher's information pack.

Figure 8.6 *Media selection steps*

Company

Product   Date

Material required

Copy and layout by   Artwork by   Copy date

Summary of advertising objectives

1. Product/service to be advertised

2. Target audience

3. Main claim

4. Evidence

5. Customer benefit

6. Response required

MEDIA TO BE USED

Media budget   Production budget

Completed by   Date

Figure 8.7 *Advertising brief*

- Improve advertising strategy.
- Determine optimum levels more accurately.
- Choose cost-effective media.
- Identify relative benefits from promotional activity.
- Improve media effectiveness by better timing.

Most firms will probably not go to the expensive lengths of econometric modelling. However, the need for a more rigorous approach remains.

The same approach needs to be taken towards promotional expenses: is there really a benefit from giving away T-shirts, pens, calendars and the like?

Operations

Cost control of production, and other operational activities, is long-established. Cost accounting, by measuring both outputs and inputs in financial and non-financial terms at each stage of production, does provide measures of productivity and very useful criteria for control purposes. However, there is growing criticism of traditional cost-accounting methods, which were based on the predominance of labour costs in most manufacturing operations, and therefore on labour hours or labour cost as the basis for allocating other costs to production units and to final products. With growing mechanization and automation, the relative importance of labour costs has decreased, calling for other methods of calculation. The increased significance of machine costs, as well as increasing overheads and research and development costs, has raised questions about the validity of product costs calculated by traditional methods. One topic currently being examined by researchers is the cost and benefit of JIT (just-in-time) inventory methods. We would refer readers to the latest professional literature on the subject, and suggest a re-examination of their cost-accounting systems.

It should be remembered that the actual provision of data to supervisors and to the workforce, can produce very positive reactions provided the report-format is meaningful. The results should be shown in productivity terms (results per production unit, or per unit of time – for example, output per man or per machine-hour, or breakdowns per day). These are meaningful terms (whereas financial data may not be), and they facilitate comparison between departments and between periods.

Quality

Quality costs have been dealt with in Chapter 6 (page 77), but we wish to emphasize the importance of setting up a system which will record these costs so that they can be analysed and used as the basis for improvement programmes. Quality costs fall into three categories:

- *Costs of failure to conform:* waste, scrap, rework, loss of sales, guarantee costs.
- *Costs of appraisal:* salaries of inspectors, product testers, etc.
- *Costs of prevention:* statistical quality control, testing of incoming materials and components, administration of supplier-accreditation programmes.

The object should be:

- To reduce the total cost of quality.
- Within the overall total, to minimize the proportion of failure and appraisal costs and to maximize the proportion of prevention costs.

We had an interesting case some years ago of the need to balance good management against practical reality. We were working for a woollen-textile manufacturer, setting up an information system. We tried to persuade the owner to agree to measure the input and output of wool at each stage of manufacture, to determine the waste at each stage. He flatly refused, without giving any explanation. Some months later, he unexpectedly reverted to the subject and agreed to the proposed system. When asked the reason for his previous refusal, he explained blithely that he had been evading tax by selling wool for cash and claiming that discrepancies in his inventory records were accounted for by waste. Had there been a system for measuring waste, he would have been unable to justify his claim to the tax authorities. Now that he had sold off all the wool he had wanted to sell, he was prepared to have the system installed.

Service

Costs of service are often inadequately controlled and sometimes result in significant losses. It is a contradiction to control production costs so closely, even though they are often not the major expense, and not control many other much more significant costs. Service costs fall into this category. They are of two types:

- *Pre-sale services* include visits to customers; surveys; preparation of proposals; etc.
- *After-sale services* include installation of equipment; teaching of customer's employees; supervision of running-in; guarantees; repairs; etc.

To ensure better control, service costs should be reclassified as follows:

- *Free-service costs,* for which no charge is made. The cost to the company of these should be known and minimized.
- *Recoverable service costs,* which are services for which charges are made, to recoup actual expenditure, but not to make a profit.

- *Profit-making services,* for which charges are levied to make a profit. Some examples are maintenance contracts on lifts and photocopy machines, provision of replacement parts, etc. These services should be treated as profit-sources and controlled accordingly.

The object of keeping separate records for these three types of service is to ensure that the costs of the first two types are kept to a minimum and fully recouped.

Support activities

These include, for example:

- Corporate headquarters.
- Financial management.
- Human resource management.
- Procurement.
- Research and development.

The number of people employed in these activities (and the associated costs) have grown enormously in recent years, increasing much faster than the number employed in production activities. Figure 8.8 shows figures for the US economy, which can be summarized as follows:

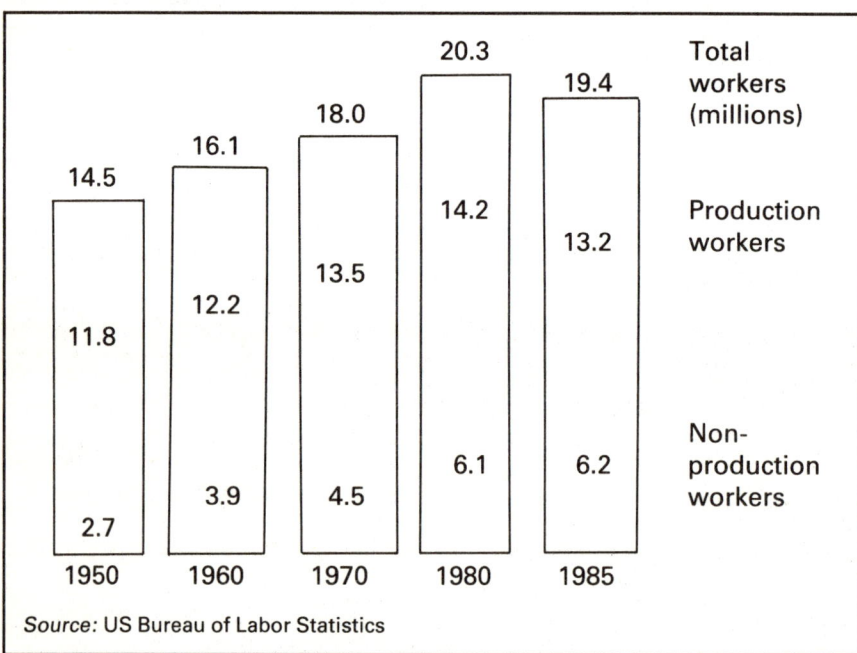

Figure 8.8 *Production versus non-production workers in US manufacturing industries*

	1950	*1985*
Production employees	82%	68%
Non-production employees	18%	32%

In America, the usual way of trying to reduce these overhead expenses has been by methods termed 'slash and burn' or 'body-count bloodbaths', whereby large numbers of people have been suddenly fired. The consequences have been serious morale problems and growing suspicion between management and the remaining employees.

Such methods are inappropriate, not only because of their devastating effect on people, but also because they do not really work. In seeking quick cost-savings, top management does not stop to conduct in-depth studies of the functions of each overhead activity and its links with primary operational activities and other overhead activities. Typical cost-cutting programmes:

- Deal with each major function in isolation.
- Fail to involve the managers of these functions.
- Fail to offer solutions for the people who have been made redundant.
- Do not change the ways in which overhead activities will be managed in the future, and thus do not prevent recurrence of the problem.

The payroll costs of non-production people often exceed those of blue-collar employees. This can be accounted for by the growing complexity of business, by the need to comply with more government regulations, and by inherent tendencies to grow. These tendencies are the consequence of the following.

- The separation of the suppliers of service (reports, analyses, etc) from the users of these services. Users often request services regardless of the cost of providing them; suppliers provide the services without knowing how they will be used or their real value.

- The professional ambitions of managers who want to be up to date with the state-of-the-art in their fields. They introduce the latest equipment and techniques regardless of cost and without thinking whether the company will really benefit.

- The anxiety of managers to please their bosses by providing services and information correctly and quickly. This leads to employing extra people 'just in case'.

In order to deal with excess overheads in a less draconian way, a method called OVA – overhead value analysis – has been developed. It is not a system, but could better be described as an approach or line of questioning. It includes the following steps:

1. *Preparing for the programme*
- Appointing a steering committee to plan the OVA programme and to monitor progress.

- Appointing and training a group of senior managers to act as internal consultants.
- Designating each non-production department an OVA unit, responsible for developing a base-line budget showing a breakdown of its annual operating costs. The unit is then required to set a budget showing a significant reduction (say as much as 40 per cent), so that the members of the unit will question every task and expense.

2. *Detailed analysis*

The manager of each OVA unit has to define the purpose of his or her unit; describe what the unit does and, in detail, its output; and estimate the true costs of that output. Analysis sometimes reveals parallel or duplicated services and activities.

3. *Generating ideas*

Joint groups of suppliers and users of services examine the data and suggest cuts. Instead of being asked what they really need, users are asked what damage would occur if certain services were discontinued. This approach identifies possible cost cuts.

4. *Review*

Proposals are submitted to the steering committee.

5. *Implementation*

Approved proposals are sent back to the OVA units for detailed planning of, and then actual, implementation.

To ensure the success of an OVA programme, the following elements are essential:

- *Relevance to strategic goals* Overhead-cutting programmes must be consistent with achieving and maintaining competitive advantage, and with the company's long-term interests.
- *Objective-setting* Cost-cutting objectives should be set very high to ensure sound analysis of current services and innovative thinking.
- *Value assessment* The value of services and products must be determined by both suppliers and users, who will jointly decide on which to cut.
- *Focus on tasks* The emphasis of the analysis must be on the results of work done, not on the people performing those tasks. The object of OVA is not to get people to work harder, but to work only on things that matter. The biggest savings come from halting unnecessary work.
- *Speed* Ideally, an overhead-reduction programme should be completed in a relatively short period (three to four months). If a programme takes too long it may cause uncertainty, insecurity and even disruption and panic.

NON-FINANCIAL FACTORS

There are many factors which contribute significantly to overall company performance but are not measured, either by the financial reporting system or by the formal system of production planning and control. We recommend that a list be prepared of all such critical factors, and that a reporting system be developed to deal with them. The list is likely to include:

- On-time deliveries.
- Production delays.
- Machine downtime.
- Customer complaints.

As an illustration of the importance of controlling deliveries, we recount the experience of one of the authors. He purchased a house 30 miles north of London and ordered various items of kitchen equipment from the local outlet for one of the large chains. The equipment was delivered, including a refrigerator which, on being plugged in, heated instead of cooled. The local shop offered to replace it, by special delivery, from a warehouse 30 miles away. The delivery truck eventually arrived, but the driver was forced to admit that, even though he and his assistant had driven 30 miles for the special purpose of delivering the refrigerator, 'they' had not loaded the item – the truck was completely empty!

MONITORING PROGRESS TOWARDS LONG-TERM OBJECTIVES

The only formal reporting system in many companies is the financial system, which functions with two limitations: it recognizes financial data only and it reports on a monthly basis. Consequently, non-financial data, which need to be reviewed at intervals which do not correspond with the month-end, are not monitored. Activities related to the implementation of long-range plans must be defined in terms of due dates ('milestones') and performance standards, and monitored by means of a non-financial control system, focusing on events and dates. The activities which should be monitored include:

- Research and development.
- Market research.
- Construction.
- Software development.

INTERPRETING CLUES ABOUT THE WORKING CLIMATE

Not only is it more difficult to measure and quantify the working climate than production and financial results, it is also more difficult to interpret the available clues.

There are events and circumstances which are important because of their direct impact on costs and output: absenteeism, lateness, labour turnover, accidents, sudden increases in wastage, machine downtime, broken tools and customer complaints. These are also important clues to change in the working climate. There are other events which may not have immediate effect on output and costs, but they are just as significant as symptoms of malaise: arguments with supervisors, complaints to shop stewards, etc. These clues must not be ignored, but investigated and dealt with promptly.

In Chapter 6 we mentioned the profiles that we obtain as a result of conducting management audits. We use these to find out which questions elicited:

- Majority positive opinions.
- Majority negative opinions.
- Significant differences of opinion.
- Significant numbers of 'no opinion' replies.

We then conduct a workshop with the employees of each unit to 'talk through' the findings of the audit. At first, the participants discuss the replies as though they express the opinions of others: 'They must have meant . . .' , or 'They probably feel that . . .' . It takes some time to get them to accept that the replies are their own. From then on, useful discussion is possible because there is no need for defensive behaviour against outside criticism. What is more, because the information has come from the employees themselves, in open discussion it is easy to reach consensus about the identification of problems and priorities in dealing with them.

THE PROCESS OF DIAGNOSIS

Diagnosis should include historical analysis, meaning the comparison, for periods past, of actual with planned results. This, of course, is based on internal figures. Sometimes, comparison with other firms is possible, and this can provide valuable information. In some branches of industry, particularly in America, inter-firm comparisons are published. In the UK, Keynote Reports are available – industry-sector overviews which provide profiles of the major companies in terms of sales, profitability and liquidity. Although only a limited number of points of comparison are given, the information is still very useful as a benchmark for other firms in the same sector.

If possible, diagnosis should also try to identify early-warning signals about future events, anticipating the development of negative trends. These could relate to sales, investment levels, undelivered orders, etc, where the pattern of historical data can suggest possible directions in the future.

In suggesting a preferred process of diagnosis, we wish to emphasize three points.

1. The process should be used as a team-building exercise, by bringing in as many as possible of those who are directly involved (both managers and non-managers).

2. Deliberate efforts should be made to familiarize non-financial people with the jargon and forms of financial reporting and analysis.

3. The process should not be a witch-hunt – looking for the 'guilty' party. It should focus on the following points:

- An objective, non-punitive analysis of what went wrong.
- Discussion on how to prevent or at least minimize the chance of recurrence.
- Discussion on 'how to get it right first time'.
- Redefinition of actions and resources necessary to achieve objectives.
- Emphasis on continued improvement.

Chapter 9

Developing Corrective Action

Dealing with identified problem areas requires corrective action of two types:

- *Doing things differently* – introducing new methods of work.
- *Modifying behaviour* – identifying behaviour which has negative consequences; defining desirable behaviour patterns; trying them out; and, most difficult of all, maintaining them.

Corrective action may be perceived as disruptive and sometimes even as threatening. To minimize negative perceptions and possible resistance, it is essential to follow a process of creative problem-solving and to develop action plans which actively involve all those people who will be affected. Task-forces should be appointed, including people from the unit where the problems exist, and from all other affected units. This is particularly relevant in cases where products, documents or data go from one part of the organization to another.

The use of such task-forces ensures the sense of 'ownership' to which we referred at the beginning of Chapter 8 – ownership both of the problems and of the proposed solutions. The process of improvement should include:

- A systematic analysis of the causes of the problems.
- A brainstorming approach to defining a number of alternative solutions.
- A rigorous method of selecting the best solutions.
- Meticulous planning of exactly how the new systems will work and how they will be implemented. Since behaviour modification is personal, it has to be dealt with sensitively and in a supportive way.

The problem-solving process should be structured so as to ensure a clear definition of the problems; collection of relevant data in a quantified form; objectivity in analysing the data and identifying the causes of the problems; and creativity in developing alternative solutions. We will now deal with the different steps in the process in more detail.

PROBLEM DEFINITION

A problem exists when there is a difference between prevailing and desired conditions. The analysis of financial data produces clear declarations: 'Raw-materials costs are too high', or 'Sales are 15 per cent down on budget'. (When actual sales exceed the budget, forecasting procedures may be inadequate, or changes of which the company is unaware may be taking place in the market.

Operating problems and problems related to the working climate are much more difficult to define clearly – too often there is a confusion between cause and effect. For example, suppose that in a discussion on deliveries to customers, two statements are made: 'Our deliveries are always late', and 'Our operators are not properly trained.' The first statement is a definition of a problem, since it is an *effect* (that is, the consequence of a still-to-be-identified cause). The second statement is a description of what might be a *cause* of the problem, and even of a possible solution. To be effective, the problem-solving process must begin with clear statements which define problems in terms which can be agreed by all members of the task-force. Furthermore, problems should be stated quantitatively (eg, '80 per cent of our deliveries to customers arrive five days late'), so that improvements can be measured.

ANALYSIS OF CAUSE AND EFFECT RELATIONSHIPS

Once a problem has been clearly defined and preliminary data obtained, it is necessary to try to identify all possible causes and to analyse the relationships between them.

Two graphic techniques have been developed to help the problem-solving task-forces in their efforts. They provide a disciplined framework for thinking and for contributing to the generation of ideas; and a convenient format and recording those ideas, facilitating analysis of cause–effect relationships and identification of the most probable causes. Both techniques are based on diagrams consisting of linked lines. Despite their apparent simplicity, completing them forces a rigorous analysis of all relevant factors.

The cause and effect diagram

This diagram is shown in Figure 9.1. The 'effect' (problem) is defined on the left-hand side of the diagram. Under category headings on the right-hand side, specific possible causes are recorded, with any possible underlying reasons for these on branch lines. In our case of delayed deliveries, the categories could be:

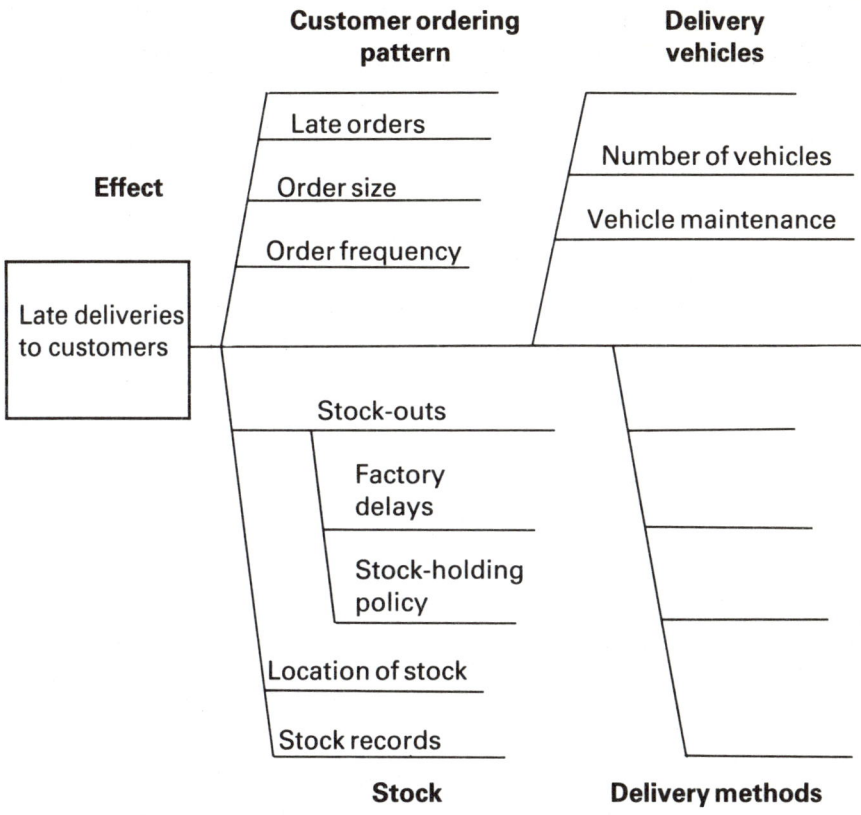

Figure 9.1 *The cause and effect diagram*

- Customer ordering pattern.
- Stock.
- Delivery vehicles.
- Delivery methods.

Contributory causes could be:

- Stock
— Bulk packaging of stock.
— Insufficient stock:
   delays in delivery from factory;
   stock-holding policy.
— Location of stock.
— Inadequate stock records.

137

Examining possible causes may lead to a reclassification of the categories; this is not undesirable, as it may lead to better understanding.

Once the cause–effect diagram has been completed, the most significant (or most likely) causes should be identified so that data on them can be collected.

The why–why diagram

This diagram, which is shown in Figure 9.2, can be used to analyse possible contributory factors to one of the causes identified on a cause–effect diagram. The why–why diagram emphasizes the links between causes and can expose points on which information is inadequate or understanding lacking.

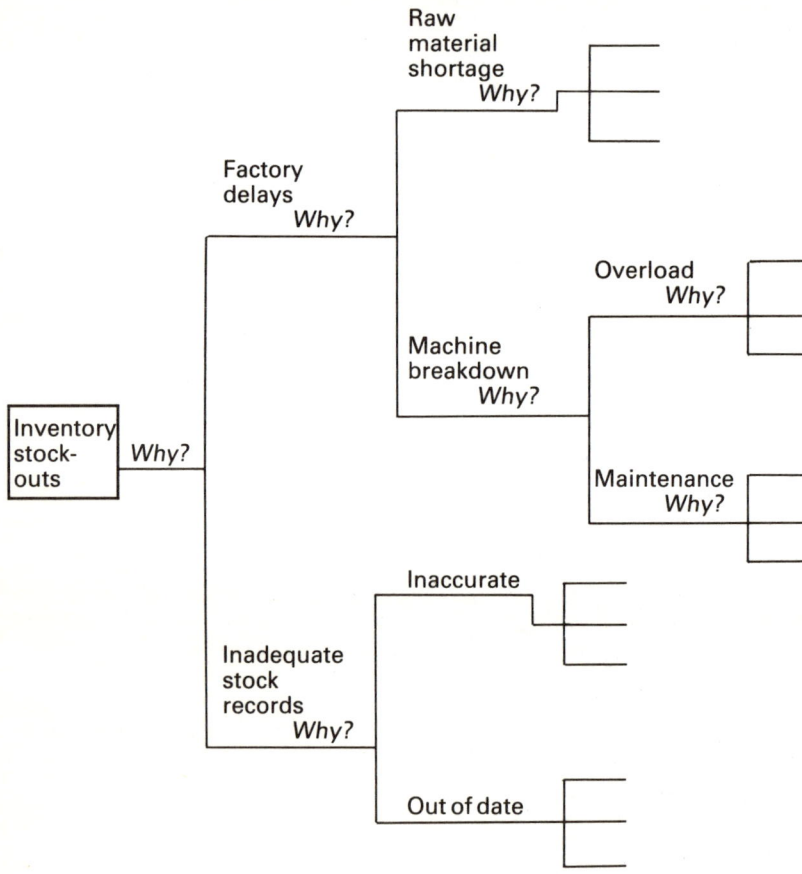

Figure 9.2   *Why–why diagram*

The selected cause is recorded on the left-hand side of the diagram. The primary reasons for that cause are recorded on branch lines, leading from the left. By repeatedly asking 'Why?', the components of each reason are identified.

DATA COLLECTION

Once the possible causes, have been identified, it is necessary to obtain relevant data. Very often, people believe they already know all the facts because of their 'experience'. However, perceptions are frequently distorted by preconceived ideas, so the only way to achieve objectivity (and minimize argument) is to obtain quantified data. The types of data required include the following:

- The size of the relevant 'population'. This, of course, does not refer to people but to the total number of events (for example, 20 000 orders per month) or items (for example, 50 000 products in the warehouse).

- Number of events, or items, in categories within each population (for example, orders of different sizes: 15 000 orders below 10 items each and 5000 orders above 10 items; or inventory items by value: 40 000 items below £5 selling price, 10 000 items above £5 selling price).

- Frequency of events (for example, 15 production-line problems per 100 products completed).

- Duration of time (for example, number of orders delayed by one day, two days, etc).

When the population is small, it may be possible to obtain data about each event or item (for example, examine every product completed). However, when the population is large, it is possible and economical to measure only a sample. To provide reliable conclusions about the characteristics of the entire population, the sample must be truly representative. Determining the appropriate size of the sample, and ensuring that all items in the population have an equal chance of being selected for examination (a random sample), call for the use of statistical quality-control techniques.

It is also necessary to provide specific answers to leading questions:

- What happened?
- How did it happen?
- Where did it occur?
- When did it occur?
- Who was involved?

The process of data collection can be made more systematic by the use of simple tools.

- Checklists are lists of questions to ask, or actions to follow (for example, checking the functioning of a product). They ensure that the investigator does not omit any essential element.

- Check-sheets are prepared forms on which observations can be recorded in a clear and systematic way (for example, waiting times, machine breakdowns, etc).

ANALYSIS OF DATA

It is necessary to organize, summarize and analyse raw data in order to draw conclusions. Statistical techniques may sometimes be required, but clear presentation of the data always facilitates analysis. Tables and diagrams showing frequency distributions are particularly useful. For example, an analysis of delivery delays could show monthly deliveries according to length of delay:

Delay (days)	Deliveries (per month)
5	10
4	16
3	59
2	10
1	5

This distribution could be presented in graphical form as shown in Figure 9.3.

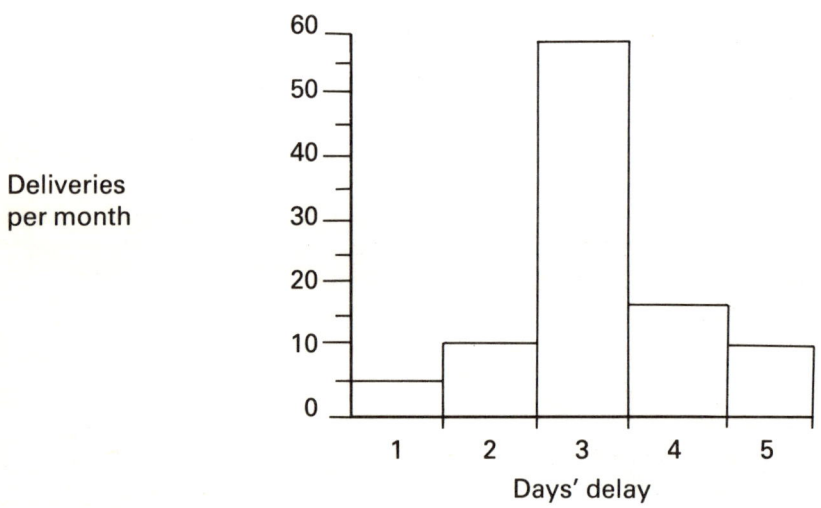

Figure 9.3 *Analysis of delivery delays in graphical form*

An analysis could be made of the relationship between the number of items per order, the number of days' delay, and the number of deliveries (Figure 9.4). From this it can be seen that the higher the number of items per order, the longer the delay. It can also be seen that 59 per cent of the delays are of three days' duration.

In trying to focus on the source of problems, the technique known as Pareto analysis can be very useful. This shows the relative importance of the various contributory factors. It is based on the Pareto Principle (also known as the 80/20 rule), which states that a very small number of contributory causes produce the greater part of the effect. For example, 20 per cent of customers produce 80 per cent of sales; or 20 per cent of items held in stock represent 80 per cent of the overall value. Applied to the problem of delivery delays, Pareto analysis produces the information shown in Figure 9.5. Thus 20 per cent of the customers (2 out of 10) place the highest number of orders per month (30), which incidentally include the highest number of items (11–15). Therefore, a method has to be developed for persuading these customers to order less frequently and to increase the number of items per order.

Items per order	Days' delay					Total deliveries
	5	4	3	2	1	
11–15	6	12	40	2	0	60
6–10	4	3	14	7	2	30
1– 5	0	1	5	1	3	10
Totals:	10	16	59	10	5	100

Figure 9.4 *Analysis of relationships: tabular form*

Items per order	Number of customers	Orders per customer	Number of orders
11–15	2	30	60
6–10	3	10	30
1– 5	5	2	10
	10		100

Figure 9.5 *Pareto analysis of the data about deliveries*

DEVELOPING SOLUTIONS

The next stage is to think of a large number of alternative ways of dealing with the defined causes of the problem. To help, the how–how diagram has been developed (Figure 9.6). This is similar to the why–why diagram but the object is to generate ideas about possible specific actions. The possible solution is recorded on the left-hand side of the diagram. By repeatedly asking 'How?', specific actions can be determined and recorded in a linked sequence.

ANALYSING ALTERNATIVE SOLUTIONS

In order to select the best possible solution from a number of alternatives, it is necessary to examine the consequences of all of them in terms of:

- Cost (investment and operating).
- Benefits (financial and non-financial).
- Possible risks.

The likelihood of the preferred solution succeeding should then be analysed in terms of factors which are likely to support its implementation and those which are likely to oppose it.

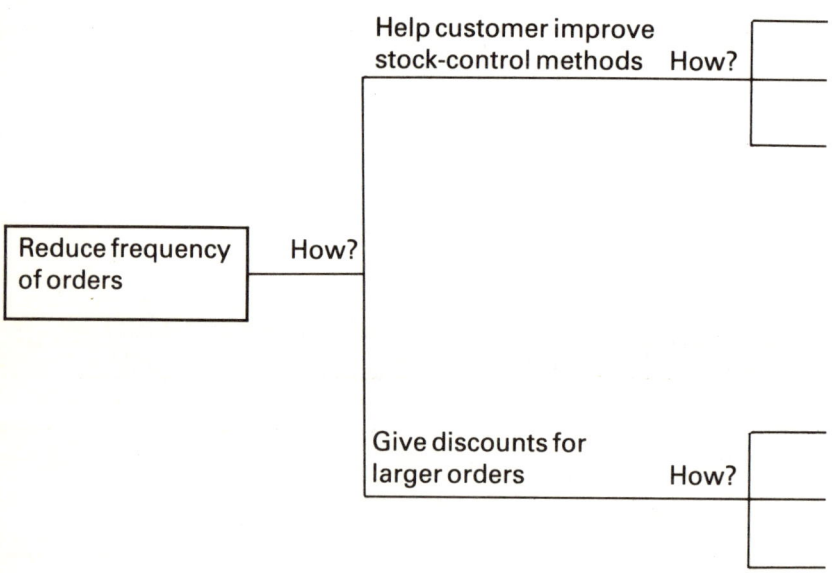

Figure 9.6   *The how–how diagram*

During the 1940s, a technique known as force-field analysis was developed in America by Kurt Lewin, an eminent social scientist, for purposes of analysing behaviour and performance. This technique has now been widely adopted as a problem-solving tool. Lewin suggested that existing condition (or situation or level of performance) is a point of equilibrium between a number of driving forces, which contribute towards improving the situation, and a number of restraining forces, which tend to inhibit improvement. He suggested that, to achieve improvement, it is necessary first to reduce the influence of the restraining forces, thus minimizing barriers to change, and then to add more driving forces. This technique can also be used to analyse possible solutions to problems. When used by a task-force, it provides a structured method that focuses on creative efforts. A force-field analysis diagram (Figure 9.7) contains three elements:

- A vertical axis, on a scale, say, of 1–10, on which current performance can be indicated.
- Downward-pointing arrows representing restraining forces.
- Upward-pointing arrows representing driving forces.

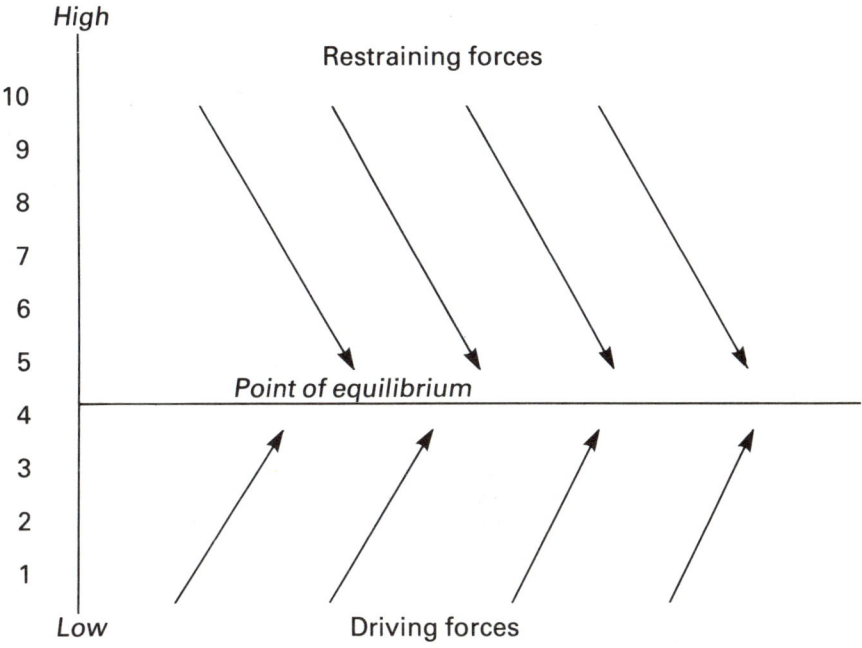

Figure 9.7 *Force-field analysis diagram*

The task-force carries out the analysis like this:

- They determine the *status quo* (current performance level, or point of equilibrium) and draw a line opposite the number on the vertical axis which, in their opinion, correctly reflects the situation.
- They define and record the existing restraining and driving forces.
- They analyse the restraining forces to determine:
  — whether they really influence the situation;
  — their relative importance: strong, moderate or weak;
  — whether they will be easy, moderately difficult, or very difficult to change.
- The identify those restraining forces which should be dealt with first, either because of their significance or because they can be tackled most easily.
- They define specific actions to eliminate, or at least reduce, these forces.
- They consider which driving forces can be strengthened.
- They identify possible new driving forces.
- They list specific actions that will strengthen existing driving forces and add new ones.

IMPLEMENTING CHOSEN SOLUTIONS

Successful implementation requires detailed planning and regular follow-up. The plans should include the following elements:

- Clear statement of problem.
- Clear statement of proposed solution.
- List of specific actions to be taken, and for each action:
  — The names of persons responsible.
  — Completion date (or dates of intermediate stages of completion).
  — Name of person who will review progress.
  — Resources required, source of each, name of person authorised to approve.
  — Measures of success.

We have observed that this team approach to problem-solving produces better analysis and decisions and is more effective in producing results than approaches where managers try to solve problems single handedly or impose solutions in an autocratic way.

We would like to end by relating the true story of a client in the shop-fitting industry, whose salesmen, production people and on-site assemblers always complained that 'the doors fall off'. The problem provided a subject for endless discussion and recrimination and yet nothing was done about it.

At our prodding (we even pointed out, unkindly, that it was possible to ensure that parts did not fall off space-craft), a task-force was appointed. Soon afterwards we asked the managing director about the problem. His reply was triumphant, 'Oh that! We solved it completely'.

Further Reading from Kogan Page

The following titles are likely to interest the reader of this book:

Don't Do. Delegate!, James M Jenks and John M Kelly
The First-Time Manager, M J Morris
A Handbook of Management Techniques, Michael Armstrong
Managing Your Time, Lothar Seiwert
The Organised Executive, Stephanie Winston
Quality at Work, D Bone and R Griggs

Better Management Skills Series

Creative Thinking in Business, C K Goman
Effective Meeting Skills, M E Haynes
Effective Performance Appraisals, R B Maddux
Effective Presentation Skills, S Mandel
The Fifty-Minute Supervisor: A Guide for the Newly Promoted, E N Chapman
How to Communicate Effectively, B Decker
How to Motivate People, T Dell
Improving Relations at Work, E N Chapman
Make Every Minute Count: How to Manage Your Time Effectively, M E Haynes
Managing Disagreement Constructively, H S Kindler
Managing Organisational Change, C D Scott and D T Jaffe
Successful Negotiation, R B Maddux
Team Building, R B Maddux

Index